The Iri

Collection

Volume One

Wildlife and Nature Writing from Ireland

Calvin Jones, Founder and Managing Editor

www.irelandswildlife.com

(As featured in Ireland's Own, The Countryman, The Irish Independent, The Irish Examiner, The Evening Echo, The West Cork Times, BBC Wildlife Magazine, Wild Ireland, Ireland's Wildlife and other publications)

ISBN: 9781520402253

Imprint: Independently published

Author's Note

I've been passionate about wildlife all my life, and writing about wildlife is a big part of what I do. This book came about as a result of a number of requests I received through the Ireland's Wildlife website and through the post from fans of my weekly back-page wildlife feature that's been running in Ireland's Own magazine since 2001.

They wanted to know if they could buy an anthology of the Ireland's Own articles in book form. The answer to that question was no… until now.

So here it is… or at least here is Volume One, with subsequent volumes coming soon. The pages that follow feature mainly the original Ireland's Own articles, but I've punctuated them throughout with other articles or columns.

I hope you enjoy the collection. If you do please consider leaving a review on Amazon to let me and others know what you think.

All the best,

Calvin!

West Cork, Ireland, January 2017

The Barn Owl (*Tyto alba*)

The barn owl will be familiar to many as the signature bird of RTE's flagship Friday night programme, "The Late Late Show". This is undoubtedly one of Ireland's most striking birds, but unfortunately the Barn Owl's ghostly silhouette and its characteristic rasping shriek are becoming increasingly scarce in Ireland.

Adult barn owls are 33 – 39 cm (13 – 15½ inches) long with a wingspan of 80 – 95 cm (31½ – 37 ½ inches). They are a beautiful orange-buff colour with grey mottling above and either pure white or white with slight buff marking on the underside. The distinctive, heart-shaped face is also white, as are the long legs, an adaptation to hunting small prey in long grass.

Barn owls are specialist hunters superbly adapted to catching small ground-dwelling mammals – although should the opportunity arise they will also take small birds, bats, reptiles, amphibians and large insects. Their principal prey depends on the area in which they hunt: close to farm buildings and outhouses they feed mainly on the house mouse (*Mus musculus*) and the brown rat (*Rattus norvegicus*), out in the open countryside, away from buildings, their diet tends to consist mainly of the wood mouse (*Apodemus sylvaticus*).

Rough grassland and field margins are the barn owl's preferred hunting habitat, and support large numbers of their rodent prey. A barn owl will typically quarter a suitable area of ground until it detects the sound of a foraging rodent in the grass below. As it flies above its prey the large, heart-shaped facial disc acts like a mini satellite dish, channelling the slightest sound to the bird's extremely sensitive ears. Barn owls have exceptional hearing and can pinpoint the position of a mouse in complete darkness purely from the tiny sounds it makes.

Once caught and killed the prey is usually carried to a favourite perch where it is swallowed whole. The indigestible parts – fur, bones and teeth – are regurgitated some time later as large, blackish pellets that accumulate at nesting and roosting sites.

Barn owls live alone or in pairs and typically mate for life. They nest, unsurprisingly, in old barns, outbuildings, church spires and in holes in old trees. Where traditional nesting sites are scarce, but other conditions are favourable, barn owls will readily occupy specially constructed nesting boxes. The female lays a clutch of between four and seven eggs from April to early May, and incubates them for about 33 days. Young owlets have voracious appetites, and both parents are kept busy providing a steady stream of rodents.

By the time they fledge some nine to twelve weeks later each owlet is capable of consuming the equivalent of a dozen mice per night. A family of Barn owls can be an extremely effective (and free) form of rodent control, and farmers who are sympathetic to the owls, and encourage them to breed on their land, rarely experience rodent problems.

Barn owl populations in the UK and Ireland are in serious decline and have dropped by over 50% since the 1930's. Much of this decline is attributed to increasingly intensive agriculture. Rough grassland, field edges and hedgerows are all disappearing, while hay meadows continue to be converted to silage. Marginal land is being reclaimed systematically for agricultural use and increasingly sophisticated harvesting techniques and modern grain storage methods don't support the small rodent populations that barn owls rely on for food.

All of this has been exacerbated by the loss of nesting and roosting sites as old hedgerow trees are felled and derelict farm buildings are demolished or renovated. Sympathetic land management and the provision of suitable nesting boxes by landowners can help barn owl populations to recover. But more of this needs to happen, and more quickly, if we are to preserve this iconic bird as a part of Ireland's natural heritage.

Ireland's best kept wildlife secret

A giant head broke the surface and a plume of spray erupted seven metres into the air. The head was followed by the graceful arch of an enormous back and, several seconds later, by a small curved dorsal fin. It was a fin whale (*Balaenoptera physalus*), the second largest animal on earth, and this one had decided to cruise alongside us for a closer look.

There were whales surfacing all around us. We counted at least thirty animals in the immediate vicinity, with more blowing in the distance. It was a phenomenal natural spectacle. I remember thinking "it doesn't get any better than this"... and then we spotted the humpbacks.

Humpback whales (*Megaptera novaeangliae*) are the natural acrobats of the whale world. The five that we encountered were putting on quite a display. We were treated to a gamut of whale behaviour that included fin slapping, fluking (lifting the tail flukes out of the water), spyhopping (lifting the head out of the water for a look around), tail-slapping and most spectacularly of all, breaching. An astonished gasp went up from everybody aboard the boat as 30 tonnes of whale leaped clear of the water. The animal seemed to hang at the apex of its jump for an extended heartbeat before gravity reclaimed its massive bulk and it fell, twisting onto its side as it entered the water creating a spectacular splash.

This was whale watching at its very best!

Mention whale watching to most people and they will immediately think of far flung corners of the globe, like Australia, New Zealand, South Africa, Canada or Alaska. Of course there are also some superb whale watching locations closer to home, with Iceland and Norway springing to mind as perhaps the most famous in Europe. But it might surprise you to learn that there is world class whale watching available right on our doorsteps here in Ireland.

During the last decade or so the Irish Whale and Dolphin Group (IWDG), an NGO set up in 1990 to promote cetacean conservation and research in

Ireland, has been monitoring dramatic baleen whale activity off the south coast. Fin and humpback whales are returning year after year to the seas of west Cork.

Pádraig Whooley, Secretary of the IWDG, attributes the relatively recent discovery of these large whales in Irish waters to a dramatic increase in observer effort, with a nationwide network of IWDG members regularly monitoring cetacean activity from headlands around the coast. These whales, he believes have probably always been visiting the area, but until relatively recently nobody was really looking for them. This theory is backed up by former fisherman Colin Barnes, who remembers seeing the whales almost as soon as he started fishing the waters off west Cork more than thirty years ago.

Colin stopped fishing commercially in 2001 to concentrate on charter angling and diving trips. As a side venture he decided to put a few posters up locally offering trips to see the whales and dolphins that he knew were out there. He was staggered by the response.

"I was absolutely amazed by what happened next," he said. "When I put the posters up I was absolutely snowed under with demand." Colin now concentrates exclusively on running whale and dolphin watching excursions through his business Cork Whale Watch operating out of Reen Pier, near the picturesque west Cork fishing village of Union Hall.

Although there is cetacean activity all year round the arrival of large baleen whales in the area is seasonal. "It's taking a while for the message to get out there that people who are really serious about seeing whales should come here in autumn and early winter," said Colin. "Things start to get good towards the end of August. Then in September you see the first humpbacks, there are usually a lot of fin whales around then and the dolphins are everywhere. It just gets better and better generally as you move into the winter."

Locally many people still don't realise that these huge whales are just off the coast, and a lot of them don't believe it at first, but word is slowly spreading. Colin Barnes was the first dedicated whale watching operator in the area, but with demand growing year on year he's been joined by others. It's a development he welcomes, and he is actively encouraging a number of people to get involved. At present Colin works closely with IWDG members along the west Cork coast to monitor the whales' movements, but he believes that a small network of boat operators could collaborate to track whales even more effectively.

From a conservation perspective the development of responsible whale watching offers significant benefits both for whales and for people. The Worldwide Fund for Nature (WWF) promotes carefully controlled whale watching as a positive conservation tool believing that it's an ideal way of providing local communities with a sustainable economic benefit from the presence of whales and dolphins. It also contributes to public understanding and support not just for cetacean conservation but for marine conservation in general.

In Ireland the IWDG is encouraging this fledgling industry to grow in a responsible and sustainable way. It recently published a policy document detailing its recommendations for the development of whale watching in Ireland. "The reality is that whale watching is almost certainly going to become a significant ecotourism venture down here in west Cork," said Pádraig Whooley, who believes that the way the industry develops here over the next few years will be crucial to its sustainability.

The IWDG would like to see the introduction of licensed whale watching operations, a focus on quality interpretation on whale watching vessels, a coordinated monitoring programme, the introduction of a code of conduct for whale watching and a conservation levy to divert some of the revenue generated by whale watching back into cetacean conservation in Ireland.

Whale watching is one of the most popular, accessible and fastest growing sectors in wildlife tourism. Globally around 10 million people a year go whale watching, spending more than US$1.25 billion and that number is growing at an astonishing 12% per year.

There's something truly awe inspiring about these oceanic titans that at once both exhilarates and humbles you. Their grace, their power and their sheer size puts a close encounter with large whales up there with the most rewarding and memorable wildlife experiences of a lifetime. With world-class whale watching available off the coast of Ireland, it's an experience that's more accessible than you might think.

Originally published in the UK magazine
"The Countryman" in 2005

Humpback Whale (*Megaptera novaeangliae*)

Humpback whales are regular visitors to Ireland's south coast. These magnificent whales begin to appear off the coast of Counties Cork and Kerry as early as April and May and stay for a significant portion of the year before moving on to their as yet undiscovered winter breeding grounds . They are also occasionally sighted elsewhere around the Irish coast.

Adult humpbacks are large, thick-set whales that typically measure from 12 – 16 metres (40 – 52 feet) long and weigh around 30 tonnes. Coloration is dark grey to black above with irregular white pattern on the throat and belly. There are 12 – 36 throat

grooves that extend down to at least their navel. The

underside of the humpback's broad tail flukes and

both sides of its long pectoral fins (which can be up to

a third of the animal's body length) also exhibit a

varied white pattern, and the unique nature of these

markings can be used like fingerprints to identify

individual animals.

The small dorsal fin is situated two thirds of

the way down the animal's body and sits just behind a

pronounced hump. Humpbacks get their name from

their habit of arching their back before diving, an

action that serves to accentuate this hump. They tend

to stay submerged for 3 to 8 minutes at a time, but

occasionally dive for 15 minutes or more. They have

a broad, bushy blow that is up to 3 metres (10 feet)

high, and normally blow 4-10 times at 20-30 second

intervals between dives. Before a deep dive the humpback will raise its tail flukes completely out of the water.

Humpbacks belong to a group of cetaceans known as baleen whales – a description that refers to the specialised feeding apparatus used to strain their prey out of the water. In humpbacks the baleen consists of 270-400 bony plates on each side of the mouth. Each plate interlocks with its neighbour by means of a fringe of bristles forming a sieve when the jaws are closed, effectively trapping small prey inside the mouth cavity where it is then swallowed. In Irish waters these whales feed on small shoaling fish like herring, capelin, mackerel and sandeels.

In order to maximise the efficiency of their feeding the whales use a range of techniques to drive their prey into a tightly concentrated group. One of the most interesting methods is called bubble netting. One or more whales circle beneath the prey blowing a steady stream of bubbles. The rising curtain of air traps the prey, forcing it into an ever more concentrated shoal through which the whales can lunge at will.

Humpback whales are widely distributed throughout the world's oceans and migrate between their tropical and subtropical breeding grounds as far as the polar ice in both hemispheres. The north-eastern Atlantic humpbacks over-winter off the coast of West Africa and the Cape Verde islands and it is likely that the animals that visit West Cork belong to this population.

Among the most vocal of the great whales humpbacks produce a wide range of complex sounds, including the famous "whale song". Only males sing, and it is thought to play a role in the breeding process. Females give birth to a single calf every two to three years. Calves are about 5 metres (16 foot) long at birth and weigh 1.3 tonnes. Commercially overexploited from the 1800's until 1966 humpbacks are still considered endangered in the North Atlantic.

Hedgehog (*Erinaceus europaeus*)

Reports suggest that the earliest record of hedgehogs in Ireland stem from County Waterford at around the time that the Normans arrived in the 13th century. However and whenever these endearing little mammals arrived they have certainly become a firmly established native and something of a favourite with people.

Hedgehogs are 15-30 cm (6-12 inches) long and weigh between 1.5 and 2 kilos (3.5 and 4.5 lb). Their back is covered with five thousand or more short, yellow-tipped spines with brown fur covering the rest of the body. Strong muscles along their backs allow hedgehogs to curl into a tight ball when threatened, relying on their spines to protect their vulnerable head and underside.

The common name, "hedgehog" comes from their pig-like habit of rooting around in the undergrowth for food. They are quite vocal, and can be heard grunting and snuffling loudly as they forage for slugs, snails, beetles and earthworms.

Hedgehogs are solitary, non-territorial animals that are mainly active at night, particularly after a heavy rainfall when they can find their prey more readily. They have poor eyesight but a keen sense of smell and excellent hearing, both of which help them to locate food.

In spring and early summer female hedgehogs give birth to one or two litters of up to five young. At first baby hedgehogs rely exclusively on their mother's milk, but start taking solid food after about three weeks. They are fully weaned at around five weeks old.

During the summer hedgehogs sleep by day in a temporary nest of leaves, moss and grass – emerging as the light fades to feed voraciously. By autumn they will have packed on a considerable amount of weight ready for hibernation during the winter months.

The hibernation nest is usually built under a hedge, in an old rabbit burrow or even at the base of a garden compost heap. Hedgehogs carry nesting material to their chosen site and, once they have made a big enough mound, burrow into the centre and make a cosy bed to sleep away the winter.

Hibernation normally takes place between November and March or April, depending on the prevailing weather conditions. During hibernation a hedgehog's heart-rate falls dramatically: from some 190 beats per minute down to about 20. The animal's core body temperature also drops, and can get as low as 10 degrees Celsius (50 degrees Fahrenheit). It is this hibernation period that accounts for most hedgehog deaths, with an estimated 75% of juvenile hedgehogs never waking from their first winter's sleep.

Hedgehogs can live for up to five years, but few reach this age in the wild. While curling into a spiny ball provides admirable protection from natural dangers – the badger is the only native Irish animal capable of prising open and killing a hedgehog – it offers scant protection against man-made threats.

Principal among these, of course, is traffic: thousands of hedgehogs are killed every year on our roads. Other prevalent manmade killers are lawnmowers and strimmers. Most animals flee to safety at the approach of these mechanical killers, but hedgehogs rely on their natural defence and simply curl into a ball and wait – with inevitably fatal results.

Taking refuge in bonfires is another common cause of hedgehog death. To them, an unlit bonfire is similar to their hedgerow habitat, and many are unwittingly burnt every year. Still more are drowned when they fall into steep-sided ornamental ponds or water-features while taking a drink.

Despite high mortality rates hedgehogs are still relatively common, and if you venture into the countryside after dark in summer sooner or later you are likely hear the rustles, grunts and snuffles of a hedgehog foraging. If you're lucky you may even catch a glimpse of one as it searches through the undergrowth for its next meal.

Ivy (*Hedera helix*)

Ivy is common climbing shrub found throughout Ireland, its attractive green foliage carpeting the façade of old buildings, stone walls and trees. Many climbing plants support themselves by entwining themselves around the supporting structure, but ivy is different. It attaches itself to the substrate directly using short, sucker-like aerial "roots" that adhere firmly to any surface and provide support for the plant. Anyone who has tried to trim a well established ivy plant will be well aware of just how effective this method of attachment can be.

Although it is a very versatile plant and can grow well in a wide variety of conditions, ivy tends to thrive best in rich, moist soil which can be either acid or alkaline. It is very shade tolerant and grows well even if completely shaded by overhanging trees. Ivy is rooted into the ground and gets its water, minerals and nutrients through these ground roots in the normal way. The small aerial roots are used primarily for attachment, and unlike some other plants, such as mistletoe, ivy does not plunder nutrients from trees that it is attached to. Indeed, contrary to popular belief ivy rarely does any damage to trees, walls or buildings: the only real risk is from the additional weight of sometimes rampant ivy, and for healthy trees and sound walls that presents relatively few problems.

In the absence of a suitable climbing surface ivy will readily sprawl to cover the ground around where it grows, and often carpets large areas of woodland floor. This habit of sprawling has been exploited by gardeners for centuries, and ivy is frequently used to conceal bare areas of ground or to disguise unsightly structures in the garden with its luxuriant evergreen foliage. It is easy to grow, can be readily trained into almost any shape and can be clipped as required. As well as the original wild variety there are many decorative hybrids that have been developed specifically for the garden.

The evergreen foliage doesn't just look attractive: ivy is an invaluable plant for wildlife as well. It provides excellent cover for nesting birds and all sorts of dark nooks and crannies in which countless invertebrates take refuge. Ivy flowers in the autumn, and provides a rich source of late nectar to many beneficial insects like hoverflies and bees. In the depths of winter when other food is scarce the swollen black berries of the ivy ripen, providing welcome bounty for birds like woodpigeons, thrushes, robins and blackcaps.

The dainty holly blue butterfly relies heavily on ivy for a significant portion of its life-cycle. As well as providing a source of nectar for towards the end of their lives this is the primary food plant for the butterfly's summer brood of caterpillars and provides cover for the over-wintering chrysalids that will emerge as new adults the following spring.

There are references to Ivy throughout human history. It was revered by the ancients, and formed not only the "poet's crown" but also the wreath of the Greek god of wine, Dionysus. The ancient Greeks held the belief that binding the forehead with ivy leaves would ward off the effects of inebriation. Greek priests often presented wreaths of ivy to newlyweds and it has traditionally been regarded as a symbol of fidelity and friendship. Herbalists have used remedies derived from ivy leaf to treat a range of complaints, including bronchitis, whooping cough, arthritis, rheumatism, and dysentery. Extracts of the herb were also applied externally to treat lice, scabies and sunburn, while the the black berries were said to cure jaundice, kill intestinal worms and even prevent the plague.

Red Squirrel (*Sciurus vulgaris*)

The red squirrel is Ireland's only native squirrel, and perhaps the cutest member of the rodent family. This endearing little tree-dweller, with its characteristic bushy tail and ear-tufts, thrived in the large forests of Scots pine that were common in Ireland after the last ice age. In time these Scots pine forests dwindled and were replaced by deciduous species less suited to red squirrels.

Ireland's native red squirrel population is thought to have become extinct towards the end of the 17th century. Our current population of squirrels is the result of reintroductions from England and Scotland between 1815 and 1856. Red squirrels are widespread, and can be found throughout the country, although they are being usurped by the larger, more aggressive grey squirrel in some areas of the midlands and the north. Grey squirrels are North American interlopers that were first introduced into Co. Longford between 1911 and 1913, and their population is gradually spreading.

Red squirrels are between 18 and 24cm (7 and 9.5 inches) long, not including the bushy tail, which adds a further 14-20cm (5.5-8 inches) to their length. Adult reds weigh between 250 and 350 grams (9 and 12.5 ounces) and in the wild live for a maximum of 7 years. There is a great deal of colour variation in red squirrel populations with coats ranging from a warm red-brown in the summer to a dark chocolate-brown with grey in winter. Coats also vary within populations, and in any given area you could see squirrels exhibiting coat colours from almost black, through various shades of red to buff.

Large patches of conifer forest are the reds' preferred habitat, although in the absence of competition from grey squirrels they will colonise less suitable deciduous woodland. Their favourite source of food is the seeds hidden inside the cones of pine and spruce trees, which they get at by gnawing away at the cone. A forest floor littered with gnawed pine-cones that resemble apple cores is a sure sign that there are squirrels present. Reds will also eat acorns, berries, fungi, and will strip away tree bark to get at the sweet sappy tissue underneath. When food is plentiful surplus is often stored to see the squirrel through leaner times.

Red squirrels are active during the day, and sleep at night in spherical nests called dreys. Dreys usually consist of a twig frame lined with soft mosses and grass, and are built at least six metres (c. 20 foot) from the ground. Each squirrel will typically use several dreys within a home range of some 7 hectares. Squirrels are not territorial: home ranges often overlap and it is common to see several squirrels foraging in the same area of forest.

Although widespread and still relatively common, red squirrels are notoriously difficult to spot. They tend to spend most of their time high in the forest canopy, using their tails as a versatile balancing aid while traversing narrow branches and leaping acrobatically from tree to tree. The long, bushy tail is what gives the squirrel its Latin name Sciurus, which comes from the Greek skai, which means shadow, and oura, which means tail – presumably from the squirrel's habit of sitting upright, its tail curved over its back and head: literally sitting in the shadow of its own tail.

Contrary to popular belief, squirrels do not hibernate in winter and remain active throughout the year. However, when the weather is particularly bad they can stay in their dreys for days at a time to conserve energy. Red squirrels usually mate between January and March and have a litter of 1-8 (usually 3) kittens after a gestation period of 36-42 days. Only females are involved in caring for the young. When conditions are favourable red squirrels can have two litters per year.

The red squirrel's natural predators include pine martens, sparrow hawks and feral cats, although the main threat to the Irish population is the continued encroachment of grey squirrels into territories traditionally occupied by reds.

Pine martens offer red squirrels a lifeline

Recovering pine marten populations in Ireland have caused a corresponding crash in grey squirrel numbers according to new research. A three year study of forests in the Irish midlands revealed that increased pine marten numbers have resulted in the disappearance of once abundant grey squirrels and the return of native reds.

"There is a common misconception that predation is automatically bad news for prey species," said Dr Emma Sheehy, lead author of the Irish study. "However, we usually only see dramatic impacts of predators on prey species when either the predator or the prey is non-native."

Where the species occurred together DNA analysis showed that grey squirrels were eight times more likely to be eaten than reds. Grey squirrel density and behaviour makes them easier targets for pine martens, but Dr Sheehy believes non-lethal predatory influences also play a significant role in the exclusion of greys, which haven't evolved to cope with the presence of martens.

Professor John Gurnell of Queen Mary University of London emphasised the need for more research, but was enthusiastic about the results of the Irish study.

"A few years ago, no one would have predicted that, as pine martens gradually recolonise their former range, alien grey squirrels disappear, allowing native red squirrels to return," he said. "It is really exciting, especially for people involved in the conservation of both pine martens and red squirrels."

Red squirrel conservationists on the ground seem a little more cautious.

"This Irish research does suggest pine martens can help red squirrel populations recover in some circumstances," said Nick Mason, Project Manager with Red Squirrels Northern England. "That's great news, but red squirrels only replaced greys where pine marten densities were extremely high."

It is tempting based on the Irish results to advocate pine marten reintroduction as a form of natural grey squirrel control. Prof Gurnell and Mr Mason advise caution, stressing the need for feasibility studies and local stakeholder consultation. Dr Sheehy warns that reintroduction doesn't offer a "quick fix"... but suggests it could provide a long term solution to a big conservation problem.

Greys v Reds -- a one-sided contest

- Grey squirrels carry the squirrelpox virus, but are otherwise unaffected. It typically kills red squirrels within a fortnight.

- Greys are twice as heavy, live at higher densities and eat nuts and seeds before they become ripe enough for reds.

- Greys easily outcompete reds in deciduous and mixed woodland. In conifer forests reds hold on for longer, unless greys

introduce disease.

Dipper (*Cinclus cinclus*)

Dippers are amazing little birds that live around fast flowing water. They get their name not from their penchant for diving beneath the surface in search of aquatic insects, but for their habit of bobbing, or "dipping", up and down in a sort of curtseying motion.

The dipper we see here in Ireland is the Irish race of the European dipper, or white-throated dipper. The origin of it's latter common name becomes

immediately apparent when you see this engaging
little bird strutting its stuff along our waterways. Its
plumage is predominantly a sooty brown – almost
black – apart from a prominent white bib on the chest,
a chestnut-brown head and chestnut brown band
below the bib.

A squat little bird, with a short tail and swift,
low flight, the dipper resembles a large, plump wren,
and shares the smaller bird's habit of seemingly
incessant activity. It is most often spotted from
bridges or riverside paths, and spends much of its
time foraging for food, flitting from rock to rock,
periodically hopping into the water and disappearing
beneath the surface. After a few moments it
reappears, if it's been lucky with a juicy morsel to
reward it for its efforts. It's astonishing to see this
industrious little bird hop into what seem to be

dangerously fast flowing water, only to emerge unscathed on a perch a little way off. It will shake itself off, and dive right back in again.

The dipper has developed some extraordinary ways of hunting for the aquatic insects, small fish and invertebrates on which it feeds. It is equally comfortable wading, swimming or plunging to the bottom in search of food. When submerged it uses its wings to swim, and to keep it submerged as it walks along the bottom. Dippers hunt by sight, and have special white eye-lids, known as nictitating membranes, which protect the eyes while submerged.

Breeding takes place along fast-flowing streams and rivers, typically in upland areas where the birds have plenty of exposed stones to perch on. In winter, they typically stay in their breeding areas, although if the weather is particularly bad they may move down to estuaries and coastal areas.

Dippers start breeding early in the year, and often have eggs in the nest before the end of February. The nest itself is dome shaped, constructed of straw and moss in crevices under bridges, in walls or rock faces, and even behind waterfalls. Amazingly the adult birds seem impervious to the cascading water as they fly headlong through it.

The female lays four or five white eggs in the nest, which are incubated for around 16 days. Young birds fledge some 20-24 days later, and dippers can rear two to three broods per year. Dippers have a maximum lifespan of around 8 years. There are an estimated 1,750-5,000 breeding pairs of dipper in Ireland, with a further 7,000 to 21,000 in Britain.

Stoat (*Mustela erminea*)

Pound for pound the stoat is one of Ireland's most formidable predators. At only 16 to 31cm (6 to 12 inches) long and weighing in at between 90 and 445g (3 and 15½oz) this fearsome little carnivore will readily take on prey two or more times its own size.

Considered to be the most widespread member of the mustelid or weasel family, stoats are common throughout Ireland, and are often referred to here as weasels (the true weasel being absent from this country). Stoats are long, slender-bodied animals with a longish, black-tipped tail. For most of the year the fur is chestnut or red-brown colour above with a cream or white underside. In winter some stoats turn completely white except for the tip of the tail, which remains black. White stoats are said to be in "ermine", and in the past were trapped for their skins when in this state.

Stoats will readily live in any habitat at any altitude as long as there is sufficient food and ground cover. They feed mainly on rodents like field mice, rats and especially rabbits – despite the latter two being substantially larger and heavier than an adult stoat. When food is hard to come by stoat's will supplement their diet with birds' eggs, fruit and will even take invertebrates like earthworms. They tend to dislike being out in the open and hunt for prey along hedgerows, ditches and verges or through the ample cover of meadowland and marshes. Excellent hearing, sight and sense of smell help stoats to find and stalk their prey, which is normally killed with a single powerful bite to the back of the neck.

Male and female stoats live separate lives, both sexes maintain territories, and like other mustelids use scent to clearly mark out the boundaries. They defend their territories against other stoats, but during the breeding season males abandon their territorial system and roam freely in search of a mate.

Each stoat will typically have a number of dens within its territory, and will move between them periodically. Dens are typically situated in a suitably sized hollow or crevice, and in colder climates are sometimes lined with rodent fur for insulation.

Sometimes the empty nest of former prey will be used as a den.

Despite the fact that mating usually takes place in early summer, female stoats do not give birth until the following spring, as implantation of the fertilised egg is delayed for 9-10 months before the four week gestation. A female stoat will typically bear between six and twelve young, known as "kits". They are blind and deaf at birth and have hardly any fur. Kits are weaned at about five weeks, and are fully independent and able to hunt for themselves after about twelve weeks.

Food shortage is the biggest threat to young stoats, and mortality in the first year is high, with many youngsters unable to find enough food through the winter months. Other threats are owls, hawks and any larger carnivores they encounter. Although they were at one time persecuted by gamekeepers and poultry farmers, stoats are now protected by law in Ireland and it is illegal to trap, injure or disturb them in any way.

Batty about bats

It was Monday night. I sat half-watching a painful American TV show (just because it was on) and half-reading the latest updates to the Ireland's Wildlife page on Facebook, when a movement outside caught my eye.

The stretch in the evening meant that, while it wasn't exactly light it wasn't really dark either. I could still see quite clearly; mostly what I could see was that there was nothing out there. I gave up and turned my attention back to the television. Suddenly there was movement again. As I watched a tiny creature emerge from a gap between the tiles and the eaves, was silhouetted briefly against the darkening sky as it spread its delicate wings, and then disappeared into the night.

The bats were back.

After mating in the autumn, Irish bats hibernate through the winter then stir into life again the following spring. In early summer the gravid females establish maternity roosts in old buildings, attic spaces, under bridges and in other suitably undisturbed locations, where they give birth to and rear their young.

A lot of people cringe at the thought of bats – but their fears are generally unfounded: based on misconceptions rather than fact. If you get to see a bat up close, you'll soon realise they are fascinating, harmless little creatures, perfectly adapted to the life they lead, and incredibly useful to have around.

Bats in general get a bad press that is far from deserved, so let's quash a few of the more common bat-related myths right now:

- Bats don't get caught in your hair: this one has always puzzled me. Bats have one of the most sophisticated sonic navigation systems on the planet, so there's very little chance of them tangling with your hair, or with anything else for that matter.

- Bats aren't dangerous: all Irish bats are insect eaters. They don't attack larger animals and don't drink blood. They play a crucial role in keeping insect populations under control, particularly some of our more virulent pest species.

- Bats aren't noisy: while it's true most Irish bats use sound to navigate and search for their prey, these echolocation calls are generally outside the range of human hearing. They may make some audible noise at their roost sites, but even if you share your home with a sizeable bat colony, chances are you'll never hear them from the house.

● Bats don't cause problems in roof spaces: bats don't gnaw wood and don't chew electrical cables like rodents – they just hang in their roost to rest after a busy night foraging. Bat guano (droppings) doesn't cause problems either: it's made up almost exclusively of chitin -- the hard material that makes up the external skeleton of their insect prey. It doesn't smell, and disintegrates into harmless metallic-looking dust.

Bat populations in general are on the decline as roosting sites are lost to development and increased use of pesticides is both poisoning bats and robbing them of their insect prey. Ten bat species occur in Ireland, all of them protected by law. It is illegal to disturb bats or to interfere with their roosting sites in any way. Several Irish bat species are considered to be of international conservation concern.

I first noticed that we had bats sharing our attic about four years ago. I was checking something in the roof space when I spotted a small, black and brown creature tucked up in the junction of the rafters. It was a brown long-eared bat that had chosen our roof as a hibernation spot. The following summer I noticed bats leaving the roof at dusk, and counted upwards of thirty individuals exiting through a tiny gap between the slates. I suspect these were common pipistrelles or soprano pipistrelles -- our smallest and most common bat species. How many use the roof altogether I have no idea... but I'm always very happy to see them return in the summer.

A single pipistrelle, weighing in at no more than six grammes, will wolf down a staggering 3,500 or so midges, mosquitoes and other small insects every night. Without the bats we'd be plagued by much bigger swarms of biting insects on those balmy summer evening, so the bats are welcome... the more the merrier.

For more information on Irish bats, where to find them, how to identify them and how you can help to conserve them, take a look at the Bat Conservation Ireland website (www.batconservationireland.org).

Leisler's Bat (*Nyctalus leisleri*)

Leisler's bats are considered rare throughout their European range, except here in Ireland, where the species is common and widespread. The Irish Leisler's bat population is the biggest in Europe, and Ireland is a significant European stronghold for this, our largest bat species.

Although it is our biggest bat, Leisler's Bat is still quite small, with an average body length of 50-70mm (c. 2-2.75 inches), a wingspan of 260-320mm (c. 10-12 inches) and weighing between 11-20g (about 0.5oz). The fur on their body is short, thick and generally a dark gold colour: redder on the back and more yellow on the belly. The face ears and wing membranes are dark brown to black.

Bats are the only true flying mammals, and like other Irish bats, Leisler's bat is nocturnal. However it does emerge earlier in the evening than most other species, and can often be seen on the wing as the sun is setting. Summer roosts are usually situated in hollow trees or in the attic spaces of buildings. Leisler's bats may travel up to 10KM (c. 6 Miles) from their roost to feed. Like all other Irish bats Leisler's bat uses echolocation to negotiate its way through the darkness, avoid obstacles and pinpoint its flying insect prey. It emits bursts of ultrasonic sound, and listens for the echoes bouncing back from objects around it. These echoes allow them to build a sonic picture of the world around them and to navigate with precision even in complete darkness. Leisler's bats produce echolocation calls with frequencies of 18-45 Khz.

The long elongated wings of the Leisler's bat are ideally suited to high-speed flight and they feed mainly over open areas of land or water. They can sometimes be seen wheeling in to pick off moths and other flying insects that gather around the glow of illuminated street lights.

From late summer to early autumn male Leisler's bats establish mating roosts. The males defend their roost sites against other males, and fly around calling for females to join them. A single male may assemble a harem of up to nine females and mate with all of them, but fertilisation is delayed until the following spring.

Leisler's bats hibernate from September to early April in hollow trees or crevices in walls and buildings. The bats have been known to travel over 50KM (31 miles) to find just the right spot for hibernation. The following summer maternity roosts, usually consisting of 20-50 pregnant females, but sometimes reaching up to 100 females, are formed. Each female will give birth to a single baby from about mid June and the young bats are weaned after 7-8 weeks.

Like all bat species, Leisler's bat is sensitive to environmental change and bat populations in general are good indicators of the general ecological health of an area. Bat species worldwide have been in decline since the middle of last century, mainly due to loss of

roosting sites through human disturbance, destruction

of woodland habitat, and the renovation of old

buildings.

All Irish bats are protected under the 1976

Wildlife Act and by the European Habitats Directive.

It is an offence to intentionally kill, disturb, handle or

keep bats without a licence. However, you may look

after an injured bat or care for an abandoned

youngster. The European Habitats Directive also

protects bat roosting and hunting sites.

Dandelion (*Taraxacum officinale*)

Dandelions are found all over Ireland and are one of our most widespread and successful wildflowers. They grow almost anywhere; their unmistakable yellow flowers, their downy seed-heads and their familiar toothed leaves greet us from hedgerow and pasture, meadow and parkland, roadside verge and garden. The plants are at their most prolific in early spring and summer, but continue to flower and seed until well into the autumn.

Dandelions take their English name from the French "Dent-de-leon", or Lion's teeth, referring to the toothed edges of the leaves. The flower itself is linked with St Briget here in Ireland, and is called by some "the little flame of God" or "the flower of Saint Bride".

Many insects rely on the dandelion as a food source for themselves and for their larvae. Several of our native butterflies and moths lay their eggs on dandelion leaves and the bright yellow flowers, with their generous stores of nectar, are a magnet to pollinating insects like bees and hoverflies. The seed heads are also a valuable food source for seed eating birds like the goldfinch.

Dandelions are among the first colonisers of waste ground. Along with other colonising plants they help to stabilise soil conditions, attract other species into the area and pave the way for the development of a rich, stable ecosystem.

One of the aspects that makes the dandelion such an effective coloniser is its method of dispersal. The downy parasol of the seed-head is made up of myriad seeds, each suspended on an individual gossamer parachute ready to be carried away by the slightest breeze. As children, most of us have unwittingly helped the dandelion in its colonisation by collecting and blowing the seed heads.

The long central "tap root" of the dandelion is particularly effective at drawing nutrients from deep in the soil. Its leaves are packed with these valuable nutrients and, when the plant dies (or is pulled up by the gardener and added to the compost heap), those nutrients are released back into the surface layers of the soil and made available to other plants.

It may be an alien concept to most gardeners, but actually allowing dandelions to grow in the garden and harvesting the leaves as compost material or mulch is an excellent way of recycling nutrients in the soil and keeping the garden fertile.

Success as a species is the very reason that the dandelion is so reviled. Its ability to colonise new areas quickly, its incredibly prolific nature, and its ability to out-compete cultivated plants do little to endear it to gardeners and crop-growers. Many people see the dandelion as a pest to be completely eradicated, but luckily the plant is too resilient to succumb to our repeated attempts at botanical genocide.

The first part of the scientific name Taraxacum is derived from the Greek words Taraxos, meaning disorder, and akos, meaning remedy. In the past the curative power of dandelions has been advocated as treatment for a variety of ailments including liver complaints, upset stomach, bilious disorders, dropsy, dizziness, gall stones, jaundice, haemorrhoids and warts.

Other uses of the plant are also well documented. Young leaves make an excellent salad and can also be used as a green vegetable. Dried leaves are a common ingredient in many digestive and herbal drinks and are used for making herb-beer, including a dandelion stout. The flowers can be made into dandelion wine, which has a reputation as an excellent tonic, and the dried roots, when roasted and ground, make an effective substitute for coffee.

The dandelion is far from the useless weed that many people dismiss it for. In fact it is an underrated, successful little plant that plays an important role in nature. It also has many useful properties that people have exploited through the ages and continue to make use of to this day.

In defence of weeds

The very mention of them can send gardeners into spasm. Throughout summer well into autumn we fight a never-ending battle with weeds. It's a futile exercise, because we know the seeds released this year mean the weeds will be back to haunt us next spring.

Rather than attempting mass genocide in the garden, I'm a great advocate of the live and let live approach to weeds. Yes, I do my chemical-free best to stop them over-running the polytunnel, taking over the lawn and hijacking the vegetable patch... but in other parts of the garden they're left to thrive. Weeds are amazing -- it just takes a subtle shift in mindset to really appreciate them, that's all.

When you think about it weeds are simply plants we haven't cultivated, growing in places we don't necessarily want them to grow. One of the things that makes weeds so troublesome in the garden is that they are so successful. In sharp contrast to their cultivated cousins our garden "weeds" (aka native wildflowers), have evolved over millions of years to survive and thrive in Ireland's unique climate, geology and soil chemistry. They are better adapted than, and therefore outcompete, the cultivated plants we introduce into our gardens.

Most common weeds are colonisers: nature's front line troops in the battle to reclaim waste ground and bare earth. In nature these colonising plants play a crucial role, preparing and enriching the soil for a succession of longer-term species. They lay the foundation for a healthy, sustainable ecosystem. That may not always be desirable on your freshly turned flower bed... but it is pretty amazing. With a little bit of imagination and a tiny bit of effort it's a trait we can harness to benefit our gardens and the native wildlife they support.

Perhaps the biggest hurdle to overcome in this is years of conditioning we get to see weeds as the enemy: something to be eradicated and destroyed at all costs. If we can look beyond our misguided preconceptions, and start to work with nature instead of striving against it, we can strike a balance that works well for our gardens and for wildlife.

We remove nutrients from the garden all the time. Pulling weeds and harvesting crops, by definition, removes the nutrients those plants have invested in growth and development out of the garden ecosystem. Obviously we can't keep taking things out of the soil without putting something back in if we want our gardens to stay healthy. Weeds can help us to do that in a natural and sustainable way.

Weeds like the stinging nettle (Urtica dioica), the dandelion (Taraxacum officinale) and coltsfoot (Tussilago farfara) are all deep-rooted species that specialise in drawing nutrients from deep in the soil, where they are locked away from most garden plants. It's a trait that makes them very effective colonisers of nutrient poor ground. By letting weeds grow in unused corners of the garden, cutting them back occasionally, and using the nutrient-rich foliage for compost, organic mulch or liquid plant feed we can recycle nutrients back into the soil making them available to our garden plants.

Other weeds have properties that make them excellent companion plants. Native wildflowers (aka weeds) tend to be better at attracting pollinating insects, but go on to perform the essential service of pollinating our garden plants too. Some of them, like hoverflies, have larvae that feed voraciously on garden pests like aphids, helping to keep them under control naturally.

Plants like like clovers (Trifolium sp.) can form a close-growing mat -- a "living mulch" that leaves little room for other weeds. They also fix nitrogen from the air, enriching the soil for garden plants. Others, like Yarrow (Achillea millefolium), release chemicals that actively repel insect pests, helping to keep them away from our crop plants.

Finally, let's not forget the role weeds play in attracting and offering refuge to the incredible diversity of wildlife that helps make our gardens all the richer. Insects, other invertebrates, birds and mammals ultimately depend on our native plants for their survival. Some of those they rely on the most are the ones we routinely eradicate as garden weeds.

Weeds are much more than the garden pests we routinely label them as. Try making a bit of room for native wildflowers in forgotten corners of your garden and it won't be long before you start to notice more wildlife. That's good news for you, good news for your garden and really good news for your local wildlife.

Garden Spider (*Araneus diadematus*)

The garden spider, or cross spider as it's also known, is the spider that creates the familiar orb webs that adorn hedgerows and shrubs in our parks, gardens and woodland throughout the summer. Our best known orb spider by far, this widespread species is found throughout the northern hemisphere.

The female garden spider is significantly bigger than the male – often more than double his size. Females generally reach between 10-13mm (c. 0.5 inch) while males reach only 4-8mm (c. 0.25 inch). Like all spiders their body is divided into two parts and they have four pairs of legs. Garden spiders vary significantly in colour, ranging from pale yellow through brown to almost black, but they always have pale markings on the abdomen that resemble a cross, giving the species its alternative name. Newly hatched spiderlings have yellow abdomens with a darker patch in the centre.

All spiders are predatory, and the garden spider feeds on flying insects – including butterflies,

flies and wasps – that it traps in a complex, spiralling orb-web. The web is large – up to 40cm (15.5 inches) in diameter – and the sticky strands effectively snare any flying insect that touches them. Garden spiders spend a lot of their time sitting motionless at the hub of their webs waiting for a meal to arrive.

As soon as an insect gets trapped in the web the spider detects the vibration through special sensory hairs on its legs and springs into action. It wraps its victim in sticky silk to immobilise it before finishing it off with a deadly injection of venom. Once the prey is subdued the spider carries it back to the centre of the web and devours it at leisure.

The garden spider usually builds a new web every day. Before starting it eats the old web to recycle the valuable silk protein it contains, then it creates a strong silk frame anchored to the surrounding vegetation. Once that's done it produces a supporting scaffold of spokes and a widely spaced spiral of strong silk before switching to the more elastic sticky silk to produce the final tightly wound spiral.

Reproduction is a delicate affair, especially for the male spider. After all, approaching a super-efficient predator more than twice your size isn't without its risks. He waits near the periphery of the female's web until he senses she's ready to mate, then he approaches with extreme caution, plucking the web as he moves to let her know he's not food. If he triggers the female's predatory response it's all over.

If he makes it to the centre of the web he embraces the the female's abdomen and mates with her before departing again just as carefully. After mating the female retires to her retreat, where she remains until her eggs are ready to lay. Then she weaves a protective egg-sac and lays her eggs inside it before sealing it up completely. She no longer feeds, and stays with the egg sac until she dies a few days later.

The following spring the eggs hatch and the young spiderlings emerge. They gather together in tight groups at first, but after a while they produce a single thread of fine silk and trail it in the wind until they are picked up and carried away to build their own miniature orb webs somewhere new.

Garden wildlife: it's a jungle out there!

As another wildlife documentary draws to a close, I can't help looking out of the window at our back garden: the patio, the lawn, the garden wall strewn with ivy, the flowers nodding their heads gently in the evening breeze.

It all seems so quiet and mundane compared to the wondrous tropical ecosystem I've just witnessed on the screen. But first impressions can be misleading….

Our gardens support an intricate web of life that, in its own way, is every bit as complex the cloud forests of Borneo, the African savannah or the Amazon rain forest. And for the species that share our little piece of Ireland with us the life and death struggle for survival is every bit as fierce.

Your garden: a wildlife haven

Over the last several decades our gardens have become increasingly important refuges for wildlife, especially in and around our towns and cities. As human populations continue to rise, and urban areas sprawl to accommodate them, they encroach on the surrounding countryside. Many of our native species are adaptable, and adjust well to life in and around our towns and cities.

Gardens offer wildlife an alternative habitat and, for some species, like hedgehogs, badgers, rabbits, squirrels and foxes, a potentially vital thoroughfare linking areas of countryside that would otherwise become isolated.

All ecosystems, our gardens included, are defined by the species that live in them, by the relationships between those species, and by their interactions with each other and their physical environment. Outside your back door, right now, the wheel of life is turning as the plants, animals and fungi that make up your resident garden community compete for a finite pool of resources. Even a cursory examination of the life in your garden will soon reveal it to be far from mundane.

But surely there can't be that many species in our gardens, can there?

Biodiversity hotspots

It is surprisingly difficult to unearth concrete data on what must be one of our most accessible wildlife habitats. Formal scientific study on the ecology of a typical garden is scarce, which means we're forced largely to rely on personal observations and records kept and published (in print and online) by amateur naturalists and interested householders.

One particularly comprehensive record of an average urban garden in central England maintained during the 1970s and '80s recorded over 1,700 distinct species – and that specifically excluded species too small and difficult to collect or accurately identify. That study extended the accepted geographical range of a number of insect species, added eight species of Ichneumonidae (solitary parasitic wasps) and five other species of wasps (*Serphidae*) to the official British species list, and identified two species thought to be new to science.

While not all gardens are necessarily so rich in terms of species diversity it is clear that there is much more going on in the average garden than initially meets the eye. But why should our gardens contain such an array of life?

Part of the answer to that question lies in the very act of gardening itself.

Garden management: creating spaces for nature

In nature plant communities tend to progress through a series of stages known as successions, until they become what ecologists call a "climax community" containing relatively few dominant species. Left to its own devices a disused field, for example, will first be colonised by rapidly growing annual wildflowers (the "weeds" commonly found in our gardens). These will in time give way to herbaceous perennials; which will in turn be followed by shrubs; small, fast-growing trees; and finally will develop into mature woodland. Our gardening activities interfere with this natural process of succession. By weeding, planting, feeding, watering and pruning our gardens we actively maintain a contrived diversity of plant life that is often much higher than the garden would naturally support.

A 3D habitat mosaic

Gardening also tends to introduce a structural diversity rarely found in such small areas in nature. A typical mature garden will have a variety of small trees or large shrubs; extensive beds of vegetation, including flowers, ferns, vegetables and of course weeds; open areas of lawn; a patio area and often a small pond or other water feature. Our gardens are a three dimensional patchwork of varying habitats, and that patchiness encourages diversity by offering suitable conditions for a greater variety of species in a confined area.

Where these habitats meet there are areas of overlap, or ecotones, which typically exhibit higher species diversity than neighbouring habitats – a phenomenon known as the "edge effect". Thus the diversity of plant life, the patchy nature of the garden environment and our continued interference with the natural process of succession results in the garden harbouring a far greater range of species than you might at first expect.

But the number of species is only the beginning of the story. A little time spent examining your garden closely will reveal a whole new world, where species interact and compete with each other in a complex biological system, employing a wide range of strategies and counter-strategies to enhance their chances of survival.

The struggle for garden survival

Plant species form the foundation of almost every ecosystem on the planet, and your garden is no exception. All of the energy that sustains the species in your garden comes from the sun.

Plants capture that energy through photosynthesis and lock it into complex chemical compounds within their tissues. Animals and bacteria that feed on this plant matter digest some of these compounds and release some of that stored energy, using some to function, and assimilating some into the consumer's own body tissue.

In turn these organisms are preyed on by others, which are preyed on by others and so on up the many food chains that make up your garden ecosystem.

Nothing in the garden is wasted. An old rotting fence post provides food for the fungi Coriolus versicolor and a home for many invertebrates.Most species in the garden will be involved in multiple food chains, and together these chains, and the links between them, form a complex food web that describes the flow of energy through the ecosystem. Scientists have established that only about ten percent of available energy passes from each level of a food chain (known as a trophic level) to the next; the rest is either lost as heat or is locked into indigestible compounds within the prey organism's body. This means that there is an ever-decreasing pool of available energy as you move up the levels of the food chain – which generally means that each successive level can support less species and fewer individuals than the level below it.

These basic rules apply to the energy flow through any ecosystem, but of course the system is far more subtle and complex than that. Individual species can occupy multiple trophic levels in different food chains within the web, and can vary their feeding habits depending on other variables within the ecosystem, including physical conditions, like temperature and rainfall, and biological conditions, such as predation pressures or nutrient levels. Many organisms, and particularly the insects (of which there are a huge number in our gardens), can occupy different trophic levels in different food chains during different phases of their life cycles.

Winners, losers, enemies, friends

Slugs and snails are a familiar, if rarely welcome sight in most gardens. These terrestrial molluscs use their rasping tongues to graze on a variety of plant species, their nocturnal foraging causing damage to several individuals but rarely killing them outright. The relationship between the slug and the plant is an antagonistic one, where the slug or snail benefits directly at the expense of the plant. Grazing is one form of antagonistic relationship common in the garden, the others are predation and parasitism. Predators like the Wolf Spider, Ladybird and Blue Tit kill and eat numerous individual prey animals, while parasites feed on a single individual of the host species to the detriment and sometimes the death of that individual, as is common with the larvae of ichneumon wasps that develop from eggs laid by the adults within the larval stages of other insects.

Mutualism is at the other extreme, and results in both species benefiting from the interaction between them. Such relationships are much more common than you might at first imagine, and occur everywhere that the selfish pursuit of one species results in a positive, if unintended, effect on the other. A typical example of this in the garden is where bees, hoverflies and other insects visit a flower. They do so to plunder its store of nectar and pollen for food... but the adaptations of the plant mean that the insect acts as an inadvertent courier for the plant's pollen, helping it to reproduce. Similarly birds that eat the berries and fruit from our garden shrubs and trees are involved in a mutualistic relationship with the plant, where they benefit from the food, and in return provide a convenient dispersal mechanism, spreading the plant's seeds over a wide geographical area.

Other mutualistic relationships occur at a much more pervasive level than that. Many animals rely on bacteria in their digestive system to break down elements of their food, and numerous plant species have bacterial associations in their root systems that help them to take up nutrients from the soil. At its extreme mutualism can result in a species becoming totally dependant on the presence of the other for its survival, a condition known as obligative symbiosis.

Between these two extremes there are commensal relationships, where one species benefits and the other is unaffected by the interaction. In the garden, for example, when aphids feed on the sap of a strong, healthy rose plant the aphids benefit from the food, but have a negligible impact on the plant itself. As always in biological systems though things are not so clear-cut. These relationships are in a constant state of flux as physical and biological variables within the ecosystem change. Let's assume for a moment that ladybirds and their larvae prey heavily on the resident aphid population, and that for some reason the ladybird population drops off. The resulting explosion in aphid numbers could shift the relationship between the aphids and the rose plant to be a more antagonistic one. Similarly, aphids feeding on a smaller, weaker plant may have a detrimental affect on the health of the plant, and the relationship again becomes antagonistic.

Perfectly adapted

The garden offers abundant examples of specific adaptations evolved to help species exploit their particular niche in the ecosystem. Woodlice, terrestrial crustaceans more closely related to crabs and lobster than to their garden neighbours, breathe using gills that they must keep moist at all times. To conserve water, woodlice restrict their activity to the hours of darkness and retire to cool, damp retreats in the heat of the day.

Some species in the garden have developed chemical weapons for defence and attack: bees, wasps, ants and beetles boast a host of stings and chemical sprays used both to overcome prey and to defend against aggressors. Ladybirds and other beetle and bug species, along with the previously mentioned woodlice, can exude a pungent secretion to dissuade would-be-predators. Many of these species have in tandem evolved bold warning colourations so that predators soon learn to avoid them. Still other species, like certain members of the hoverfly family, mimic the colouration and pattern of more dangerous or unpalatable creatures and "piggy-back" on their successful adaptation to their own advantage. The social bees, wasps and ants, all common in the garden, live in colonies ruled by one or more queens. These colonies work collectively to meet the challenges of survival in the garden ecosystem.

And it's not only animals that are specifically adapted to their niche in the environment. Plants also have countless adaptations to improve their tolerance of desiccation, to maximise their access to light, to increase their chances of pollination, to improve their dispersal, to access the nutrients in the soil and to defend against attack.

The average Irish garden is very much alive, and, for me at least, is every bit as unique and fascinating as any other natural community. So the next time you're watching the wonders of a tropical

ecosystem unfold on your television screen, take a
look out of your window… there could easily be just
as much going on quite literally in your own
backyard!

Acorn Barnacle (*Semibalanus balanoides*)

Barnacles are a common sight around Ireland's rocky shores. These tiny animals form the familiar off-white patchwork that often covers large swathes of rock between the high and low water marks. Barnacles are crustaceans, relatives of crabs, shrimps and lobsters, although they were not firmly accepted as part of that group until as late as the 1830s. Before that the sedentary existence of the adults and their protective calcareous shells often led to them being grouped with the superficially similar molluscs.

The acorn barnacle is the most common type of barnacle found around the Irish coast, and is abundant between the high and low tide marks wherever there is suitable substrate for its larvae to settle on. Adult acorn barnacles are small, and only grow to a maximum size of about 15mm (0.6 inch) long. They have a cone-shaped shell made up of six overlapping calcareous plates with a diamond shaped opening at the apex of the cone. When the tide is out this opening is sealed by another pair of calcareous plates that serve to protect the animal from the lethal drying effects of sun and wind.

Barnacles feed on zooplankton – tiny free-swimming creatures that live in the water column.

Once submerged by the incoming tide the adult barnacle retracts the plates sealing the opening and extends feathery legs called "cirri" into the water. If there is a current present the barnacle simply holds the cirri fully extended, letting them filter passing food out of the water. In the absence of a current the barnacle will create its own by rhythmically beating the cirri to induce water movement.

High plankton levels associated with spring and autumn herald a feeding bonanza, and most barnacle feeding activity is concentrated into these two seasons. In contrast they hardly feed at all through the winter when plankton levels are severely depressed.

Like all other crustaceans barnacles need to shed their skin to accommodate growth. In barnacles the rate of growth is directly related to feeding and temperature, so the frequency of the moult is variable. Because barnacles lower on the shore have more time to feed during each tidal cycle they tend to grow more quickly than those higher up the shore, and consequently need to moult more often.

Acorn barnacles are hermaphrodites: each individual contains both male and female reproductive organs. Despite this each individual acts as either as a functional male or a functional female. Mating takes place in November and December, when functional males will fertilise the eggs of numerous functional females in their immediate vicinity. The fertilised eggs are stored in the barnacle's body over the winter, where they develop into larvae called "nauplii".

These nauplii are released into the water column between February and May to coincide with the annual spring algal bloom, ensuring that there is a ready source of food available to them. The nauplii spend several weeks feeding in the water column where they undergo a series of six moults before developing into a second larval form known as a "cyprid". The cyprid is specialised for seeking out a settlement site, and searches the substrate using its antennae. Once it has identified a good site the cyprid fastens itself to the rock and undergoes a metamorphosis into the adult form.

Much of our current knowledge about barnacles is based on the definitive work of eminent biologist Charles Darwin, who dedicated eight years (1846-1854) to studying them. It is likely that this extensive study of barnacles had a significant influence on the development of Darwin's seminal theory of natural selection that he published in 1859.

Basking Shark (*Cetorhinus maximus*)

The basking shark is the biggest fish found in Irish waters, and the second largest fish on earth after its Indo-Pacific cousin, the whale shark. Although it belongs to the same family as the notorious great white, and has more teeth than any other shark, the basking shark is actually a gentle giant. It's a filter feeder, and exists on tiny creatures that it sifts out of the plankton (a rich soup of tiny plants and animals that live in the surface layers of the ocean) through specially adapted gill slits.

Basking sharks can be found in temperate seas throughout the world with an average temperature range of 8°-14° C. They have been recorded in the Pacific, Indian and Atlantic oceans and can be seen off the Irish coast during the summer months. They are huge fish, with specimens reaching lengths of up to 12 metres (39 feet) and weighing up to 7 tonnes.

Basking sharks are grey-brown to charcoal-blue above with a pale belly. A distinctive bulbous snout combine with the massive gape, huge dorsal fin, large crescent-moon tail, long pectoral fins, and five huge gill slits each side of the head to make the basking shark unmistakeable.

Little is known about the natural ecology and behaviour of these extraordinary fish. Basking sharks get their common name from their feeding behaviour. They move through the water so slowly that they look like they're basking on the surface. What they're actually doing is filtering water... lots of it.

Basking sharks are passive feeders. They don't actively hunt their prey, they simply swim through the water with their mouths open wide. Water enters through the open mouth and is expelled via the enlarged gill slits across a large number of structures called gill rakers, which act as an effective filter retaining the shark's planktonic food.

A shark will typically swim with its mouth open for 30 to 60 seconds, then close its mouth to swallow the filtered plankton before starting the process over again. Estimates suggest a fairly large basking shark will filter around 1,500,000 litres of water per hour.

Although normally solitary, basking sharks are sometimes encountered in small groups, and very occasionally in larger aggregations of 100 individuals or more. They disappear from coastal waters over the winter. Exactly where they go is unclear, but they are thought to migrate offshore to deeper waters. They return to the coast in spring to feed and to find partners for mating.

Basking sharks are thought to reach sexual maturity at between 12 and 20 years of age. Baby sharks are live-bearing, with young developing from eggs inside the female's body and hatching just before they are born. The gestation period of basking sharks is unknown, but is estimated at anywhere between 12 months and 3 years. Pups are 1.5 to 2 metres (5 to 6.5 feet) long at birth.

Because they grow slowly, mature late, and have a slow rate of reproduction basking sharks are very susceptible to human exploitation. In the past the species was heavily fished for the oil in their huge livers, and a booming basking shark fishery operated out of Achill Island in Co. Mayo. The last basking shark was landed commercially in Achill as recently as 1984.

Today the main threat to the species is the trade in shark's fins fuelled by the increasing demand for shark fin soup in East Asia. The basking shark's 2 metre (6.5 ft) dorsal fin has unfortunately become a valuable commercial prize.

Emperor Moth (*Saturnia pavonia*)

The adult emperor moth is a truly spectacular insect. On the wing in April and May, the male of this large, day-flying moth species is a particularly striking sight, and can easily be mistaken for a butterfly due to its bright colours. It is a fairly widespread species, one that favours open scrub habitat on heathland, moorland, fens, along field margins and hedgerows, woodland rides and sand dunes.

This is a large moth, with females reaching a wingspan of 35-41 mm (1.22-1.61 inches). Male's, which are slightly smaller, reach 27-32 mm (1.06-1.26 inches).

What the males lacks in stature, though, they more than make up for in the colourful splendour of their markings. On the upper fore-wings the pattern consists of grey, dark brown and orange or pinkish markings, with prominent black and yellow eye spots, reminiscent of the eyes of an owl. The upper hind-wings carry similar eye-spots, these set against an orange background.

The female moth also has prominent eye-spots on the wings, but lacks the male's more colourful markings. Instead the eye-spots are set against a background of buff, grey and white patterns. The thorax in both sexes is covered in long hairs.

For the few months that they are on the wing adult emperor moths do not feed at all. Their sole purpose is to find a mate and reproduce. While butterflies locate their mates by sight, moths on the other hand – even day-flying species like the emperor – use smell to locate their partners. The newly emerged female moths release a unique chemical signature – a pheromone – that is irresistible to male emperor moths. All they have to do is wait for potential suitors to follow the scent trail and come to them.

Males, in contrast, fly around rapidly, zigzagging across the breeze trying to pick up the slightest hint of the female pheromone. They can detect it at up to a kilometre away, and just a few molecules collected in their feather-like antennae are enough to set them on a course towards their prospective mate. Males have to hurry, however, as competition for females is fierce, and the first male to arrive has by far the best chance of mating.

Once mated, the female takes to the wing and starts laying her eggs in batches on any of the various food plants that emperor caterpillars eat. These including familiar plants like meadow sweet, heather, hawthorn, bramble and birch. The newly hatched caterpillars are black and hairy, and tend to mass together for mutual protection at first. As they grow they gradually spread out and eventually disperse completely.

By the time they are fully grown the caterpillars will have turned bright green with black bands, and have yellow, pink or orange bumps on them. Each of these bumps sports a tuft of short black hairs. Once they are large enough the caterpillars that survive spin themselves a silk cocoon, in which they pupate. The cocoon has an interesting one-way exit system: a ring of stiff outward-sloping bristles that makes it easy for the emerging moth to push its way out, while at the same time preventing unwanted intruders from entering.

Inside this protective silk casing the pupa spends the winter. The following spring, it's metamorphosis complete, it emerges as an adult moth to begin the whole process all over again.

Common Frog (*Rana temporaria*)

Of the three species of amphibian found in Ireland the common frog is by far the most familiar. Most people think of frogs as aquatic creatures, but in fact they spend most of their lives on land, only returning to the water in order to breed.

Adult frogs are from 6-10cm (2.4-4 inches) long. They are smooth skinned, tailless amphibians with powerful hind legs that are particularly well suited to jumping. The upper surface of the skin is variable in colour – ranging from a light yellowish brown to dark olive green. Some individuals even have a reddish tinge and almost black animals are not unheard of. Most animals exhibit a variable pattern of black or brown marks on the back and the species has a very distinctive brown patch behind each eye.

On the underside males tend to be a dirty white or pale yellow while females vary from pale yellow to orange. There are often brown speckles present in both sexes. Males tend to be slightly smaller than females and can be distinguished by the dark bluish-black nuptial pads – which are swellings on the first finger of their forelimbs. These swellings become much more pronounced during the breeding season and help the male to get a firm grip on the female's smooth skin during mating.

Depending on the weather common frogs begin to emerge from hibernation in February or March and head straight for their freshwater breeding grounds. Males usually arrive before females and start croaking to attract a mate. Once females start to arrive the males start croaking in earnest and wrestle with each other to gain access to a potential mate. After overcoming his rivals a successful male will clamp himself to her back using his nuptial pads in a mating embrace known as "amplexus". They may stay clamped together like this for days before spawning.

Eventually the female will lay 1000 to 4000 eggs which are fertilised by the male as they are released. This frog's spawn floats in clumps protected by a jelly-like coating until the tadpoles emerge after 30-40 days. The tiny tadpoles feed on the remains of the frogspawn for the first two days before they switch to a diet of algae. As they grow bigger they also start to include aquatic insects in their diet. Hind legs develop at between six and nine weeks, the tadpoles lose their feathery gills and develop lungs – forcing them to the water's surface to gulp air. Front legs are fully developed by about 11 weeks and the tail begins to be absorbed. At 12 weeks the metamorphosis is practically complete and the tiny froglet will leave the water, spending most of its time hiding in the vegetation on the water's edge.

Frogs don't feed during the breeding season, but once breeding is over they will eat practically any moving invertebrate that crosses their path, catching their prey with their long, sticky tongue. Adult frogs feed almost exclusively on land, but youngster frogs will also forage in the water. Although they are often seen by day frogs tend to be more active by night.

In winter frogs hibernate beneath compost heaps, under stones and logs or buried in the mud at the bottom of a pond where they survive by extracting oxygen from the water through their skin. They will not emerge until breeding time comes around again the following spring.

Otter (*Lutra lutra*)

Ireland is considered to have the healthiest otter population in Europe. Surveys show that otters are present in more than ninety percent of our inland waterways and coastal waters. The species, already extinct over much of its former range, is listed as "vulnerable to extinction" by the IUCN (International Union for the Conservation of Nature) and the thriving Irish otter population is of international importance in terms of otter conservation.

Despite being widespread, and in some areas locally common, the otter is an elusive and secretive animal that is rarely seen. Superb eyesight, an acute sense of smell and exceptional hearing usually give the otter plenty of warning when people are around and it tends to stay out of sight. Even people studying otter populations rely heavily on the readily recognisable signs of their activity and consider themselves lucky to catch a glimpse of their subjects.

Otters are between 55 and 130 centimetres (22 to 51 inches) long and typically weigh between 5 and 12 kilos (11 and 26 pounds), with dog otters slightly larger and heavier than the bitches. They are the only truly amphibious members of the weasel or mystelid family, and are superbly adapted to the aquatic life they lead.

Their long, sleek bodies; short, powerful legs; webbing between the toes and strong, rudder-like tails combine to give otters tremendous propulsion and exceptional manoeuvrability in the water. When diving otters close their ears and nostrils to keep water out, and their coat keeps them dry and warm in even the coldest conditions. The coat, chestnut brown in colour and slightly lighter on the belly, is actually made up of two distinct types of fur. A thick outer layer of waterproof guard-hairs covers a very dense, fine under-coat which provides much needed insulation.

During the day otters sleep in a burrow known as a holt, usually situated under tree roots or another suitable location on the banks of a lake, river or stream. At dusk they emerge to hunt their favourite food. Otters eat mainly fish, which they actively chase underwater using both sight and their long, sensitive whiskers to detect their prey. They also take crustaceans, small waterfowl, frogs and small mammals. Once a meal is caught the otter will usually return to dry land before consuming it, and food remains are one of the regular signs of otter activity used by scientists to monitor populations. Another commonly encountered otter sign is their spraints or droppings.

Spraints are usually deposited regularly at specific sites as territorial markers, and provide an array of useful information to other otters in the area. They are cigar shaped, about 3 to 10 centimetres (1 to 4 inches) long and are tarry and black or dark green in colour when fresh. They have a very distinct musty odour that is often described as like newly mown grass or jasmine tea. As they age the spraints fade to grey, but retain the distinctive odour.

Otters breed once every two years, as the cubs remain dependent on their mothers for the first year of life. Breeding can take place at any time of the year, and after a period of nine weeks gestation one to four cubs will be born in a nest of straw and weeds within the holt. Blind at birth and covered in a warm downy fur, the cubs eventually open their eyes at around 35 days old, but will stay in the holt for another few weeks before they start to venture forth under the watchful eye of their mother. Otter cubs are weaned onto solid food after 3 to 4 months, but stay with their mother for the first 12 to 15 months of their lives.

While the Irish otter population is healthy at present, current downward trends in our water quality, increasing human encroachment along our waterways and rising levels of pollution are all worrying signs. Let's hope that these trends will be reversed soon, for the otters' sake and for our own!

Otters: a breathtaking wildlife experience

It was a day that I should have spent in the office working… but the forecast for the rest of the week was bad. This was the only weather window to get out around my local patch. Decision made I grabbed my binoculars and headed out.

You never really know what to expect when you leave the house in search of wildlife. That sense of anticipation is like a drug… it heightens the senses and means you're more tuned in to things around you.

If you keep your eyes and ears open you really never know what you might see.

Today turned into a bit of an impromptu mammal-fest. Things got off to a great start when I found a badger print on a muddy farm track. I know there are badgers around the patch, but it's always great to see confirmation they are still here. Getting to see the animal itself is another matter. I still haven't seen a badger on my local patch — something I'll need to remedy over the coming year.

There were lots of fox signs around too — tracks, fur snagged on barbed wire, that distinctive musky fox aroma and of course that regular fox "calling card" — poo! This wasn't unexpected: there are a lot of foxes around at the moment. We're entering the breeding season, and males are abroad searching and competing for females. I spotted five the other night in one field, directly across from the house, illuminated by the remarkable Fenix PD35, a pint-sized powerhouse of a torch I'm currently testing.

So, plenty of foxes — and no shortage of fox food in the form of rabbits. Rabbit populations around here tend to fluctuate — building to ridiculous numbers, then crashing completely, before slowly building again. At the moment they're on the rise, and there are lots of rabbits along all of the ditches and hedgerows, and plenty of rabbit signs… tracks, poo, burrows and signs of digging all over the place.

Traipsing across a wet field I flushed a group of snipe — there must have been around 30 of them hunkered down in this one soggy patch of pasture.

They stayed completely hidden until I was almost on top of them. One broke and took flight, then another, and suddenly the grass in front of me erupted as the rest took to the air, calling noisily as they zig-zagged into the distance. They're always lovely birds to see — and you don't often get to see that many all at once.

I made my way along the edge of the marsh and over to a small flooded quarry I only discovered last autumn. I've been checking it regularly since. — it has steep, ivy and shrub-strewn sides dropping to the water on three sides, and an overgrown, but more shallow approach to the water on the other — which means that while there's no access for people, there is a way in for animals.

So far the only things I've seen here are kestrels, chough, the usual suspects on the small birds front (tits and warblers and the like), and mallard on the pool itself. I'm hoping it might attract a kingfisher at some point… assuming there are any fish in it of course… fingers crossed.

Leaving the quarry I made my way down to the road that follows a stream running out of a nearby lake. The stream fluctuates between shallow, fast-flowing rapids and deeper meandering sections. Following the road I kept one eye on the stream, the other on the scrub and pasture either side of the road for signs of life. A high pitched whistle caught my attention, then a dark arching back in the middle of the stream — an otter! Another back appeared… two otters!

I couldn't believe my luck. I've seen signs of otters on the patch before — otter "slides" from the bank into the stream, the occasional sprainting site and otter tracks. Once I saw a large dog otter at a distance on the lake at dusk, but to see two close up in broad daylight like this was a rare treat. Luckily I was downwind, and they continued porpoising in mid stream completely oblivious to me.

Following the road I stayed with them as they made their way upstream, hunting as they went. Occasionally they would climb out onto the bank, then slide gracefully into the water again. One — the larger of the two — seemed to be taking the lead, the smaller following, calling to each other with that high-pitched, whistling call. From their behaviour I'm guessing this was an adult female and one of last season's kits.

At one point the larger otter caught a fish — a medium-sized trout it looked like — and took it up onto the grassy bank. The smaller otter followed and noisily attempted to claim a share of the prize. They quarrelled noisily, then slipped back into the water to continue their leisurely journey.

It seemed like I was with them for ages. At times the road looped away from the stream, and I hurried ahead, worried I'd lose them while they were out of sight. I was always conscious the wind could carry my scent their way and spook them. But my luck held… they always reappeared, making their way steadily upstream. At their closest they were no more than twenty feet away from me.

Had I brought the "proper" camera with me I'm sure I'd have captured some outstanding images.

But on a walk around the patch I often choose to leave it at home — travelling light, enjoying watching the wildlife rather than worrying about the perfect shot. Today though I was kicking myself for leaving it behind. I had to make do with my mobile phone and my binoculars — a poor photographic substitute, but the best available. I snapped away and hoped for the best!

Eventually the mother otter caught sight of me, sounded the alarm and they disappeared under a small bridge and didn't re-emerge. I waited for a few minutes, and then left them alone. I'd been with them long enough.

I was literally buzzing with excitement. The half-hour or so I spent with these remarkable creatures ranks as one of the most amazing wildlife encounters of my life. That includes coming face-to-face with a wild male orangutan in the rainforests of Borneo, watching killer whales off the coast of British Columbia, and breaching humpbacks just off West Cork. It was an unforgettable wildlife moment… and it happened right on my doorstep.

That evening I spotted them again, up at the lake, this time sharing the experience with my 10-year-old daughter. They were further away, and the light was fading, but it was still a magical encounter. I'm hoping they'll decide to stick around, and that I'll be lucky enough to catch up with them again soon.

The Red Fox (*Vulpes vulpes*)

The red fox, one of Ireland's largest land predators, is common throughout the country in both rural and urban habitats. Elusive, and largely nocturnal, the fox usually stays well hidden and many people, particularly in our cities, go about their lives completely oblivious to the proximity of this striking mammal.

Adult foxes grow to around a metre (3.28 foot) in length and weigh between five and seven kilos (11-15.5 lb), with the dog fox being slightly larger and heavier than the vixen. In captivity foxes can live for up to fourteen years, but the average lifespan of wild adults is much less. The breeding season starts in December and peaks around the end of January and start of February. During this period foxes are more active during the day than normal and are generally seen more frequently by people.

The fox's earth can be found in a variety of habitats, but a favourite rural location is at the periphery of woodland where there is plenty of cover and easy access to both the wood and to the open pastures beyond. Occasionally foxes will occupy old rabbit warrens or badger sets to rear their young.

On average four to five cubs are born around March onto the bare soil of an underground chamber down in the earth. The young are born blind and covered in short chocolate-coloured fur. Their eyes open at around two to three weeks old, and at first are a slate-blue colour, changing to brown or amber at about four to five weeks. This coincides with the start of a change in coat colour, the chocolate brown gradually changing to the more familiar red -- although individuals can vary greatly in colour, with some remaining quite dark for life. By this time the inquisitive cubs have started to explore outside the earth, first on wobbly legs, but becoming increasingly steady and bold as the weeks draw on. They begin foraging for food around the entrance of the earth and will take the odd beetle, earthworm or slug if the opportunity presents itself.

Although foxes have no natural predators many die young through a combination of disease, shootings, fox-hunting and other factors. A particularly big killer is traffic, and large numbers of foxes die every year on our roads. Death rates are particularly high during the breeding season, when foxes wander more widely and are generally more active, exposing themselves to more risks. Another period of high mortality is during April and May when the adults are struggling to feed a hungry litter of cubs, the increased activity again exposing the adults to more danger.

Despite high mortality rates the fox remains an incredibly successful animal, and is one of the opportunist champions of the animal kingdom. Foxes thrive in urban environments the world over, and take full advantage of our wasteful existence to eke out a very satisfactory living in our cities. Urban fox populations are often denser and more prolific than their rural counterparts, thanks largely to a surfeit of food available in urban surroundings. Scavenging is much easier than hunting for a living and urban foxes are extremely successful scavengers.

In rural communities foxes often get a bad name for attacking livestock, and while it is true that a fox will feed on a dead sheep, or will carry away a dead lamb if it comes across one, there are few substantiated claims of foxes taking healthy livestock. On the Isle of Mull in Scotland, where there are no foxes, records show that rates of lamb survival are no higher than those of the mainland, where foxes are common. Similarly the fox that takes chickens or ducks is only acting on a predators instinct to avail of the most easily available food source.

Tales of the fox as a ruthless killer that slaughters for enjoyment are also greatly exaggerated. Any predator, when confronted with an abundance of prey animals (such as a fox will encounter in the chicken coop) will instinctively kill multiple animals, and, if left undisturbed, will then return to recover each of them and will cache them for retrieval in harder times ahead. When the fox is disturbed it makes a swift exit, leaving several dead birds behind it, and earning its unjustified reputation. Ultimately foxes are only doing what comes naturally to any predator, and it is up to people to protect their poultry in secure accommodation at night when foxes are present.

Foxes are a wonderful part of our natural heritage, and, in spite of high mortality and often unjustified persecution, are adaptable and successful enough to remain so for many years to come.

Bracken (*Pteridium aquilinum*)

Most of us are familiar with the long,

branching fronds of bracken. This common deciduous

fern is found all over Ireland and grows in all sorts of

habitats. It is a large fern: fronds often grow to 2

metres (6½ feet) or more and have been known to

reach 3 metres (10 feet) in favourable conditions.

The species' scientific name (Pteridium

aquilinum) comes from the Greek word Pteris, which

means fern, and the Latin aquilinum, which means eagle-like. Bracken is an old-English word that originally applied to all large ferns, but eventually came to represent this species in particular. It has a variety of other common names, including brake-fern, eagle-fern and fiddlehead – a reference to the curled young fronds that have been likened to both the head of a fiddle and a shepherds crook. Young shoots and leaves are covered in a downy, silvery hair and brown scales that gradually fall away as the young frond unfurls.

The fronds are made up of a number of lance-shaped leaflets or pinnae that grow out of the central leaf-stem. Each leaflet is further divided into smaller sub-leaflets or pinnules. Fertile fronds bear brown spore-filled fruiting bodies called sori on the underside of these pinnules.

Bracken fronds die off after the first frost of winter, rapidly turning brown and falling to the ground. New fronds emerge again the following spring when all danger of frost has passed.

The visible fronds are attached to a thick root-like underground stem called a rhizome. Rhizomes can be up to 2cm (1 inch) thick and extend up to 6 metres (20 feet). They generally consist of an elongated main stem that acts primarily a carbohydrate and water store, off which a series of sub branches extend closer to the surface and support the fronds. On the underside of the rhizome thin, brittle black roots extend into the soil to extract water and nutrients.

Bracken is a well adapted pioneer species that colonises quickly by means of its wind-borne spores.

Once established it expands rapidly via a creeping underground network of rhizomes. This can result in large colonies of bracken that completely dominate the immediate landscape. It is a domination assisted by an impressive array of complex chemical compounds that allow bracken to inhibit the growth of competing plants, discourage grazing animals and disrupt the growth patterns of insect pests.

People have used bracken throughout recorded history. The fronds have been used as packaging material, animal bedding, roofing thatch, green manure and fuel. In the Middle Ages bracken was considered so valuable that is was sometimes used to pay rents. Ash from bracken fronds was used as a source of potash in the soap and glass industries until the 1860's and the rhizomes were used in tanning leather and to dye wool yellow.

Bracken was also a source of food: the newly emerging fiddleheads were picked and consumed fresh or preserved by salting, pickling or sun-drying. Both rhizomes and fronds have been used in brewing beer, rhizome starch has been used as a replacement for arrowroot and dried, powdered rhizome has been used to make bread. In some places, most notably Japan, bracken is still used as a source of food.

However, the wisdom of eating bracken has to be called into question as every part of the plant is toxic. It is poisonous to livestock, and if eaten in sufficient quantity can prove fatal. Eating bracken has been associated with increased instances of stomach cancer in humans, and the plant has been implicated in certain types of leukaemia, bladder cancer and cancer of the oesophagus.

Chemical warfare in the Irish countryside

As you read this article a complex arsenal of chemical weapons is being manufactured at sites all over the island of Ireland. When deployed these chemical agents are designed to subdue, inhibit, mutilate, mutate and in some cases even kill!

The manufacturers of this nationwide chemical stockpile are of course plants. Unable to resort to the physical "fight or flight" response that's open to most animals, when danger threatens plants have developed alternative strategies in the battle for survival.

All plants manufacture complex biochemical substances for their basic existence. They need some of theses chemicals to synthesise food, to breathe, to grow and to reproduce, but plants are also crammed with chemicals that play no discernable role in their everyday biochemistry. These "secondary" chemicals range from relatively simple poisons like oxalic acid and cyanide, to more complex molecules like glycosides, alkaloids, terpenoids, saponins, flavonoids and tannins.

Perhaps the most obvious example of chemical weaponry employed by an Irish plant is the familiar defence of the stinging nettle (*Urtica dioica*).

The painful sting is delivered via hollow silica hairs on the leaves. Brittle at the tip, these hairs break at the slightest touch and act like tiny hypodermic needles to deliver their payload of venom. Nettle stings were once thought to be simply formic acid, but detailed analysis has revealed that the main chemicals involved are histamine, acetylcholine, serotonin and another as yet unidentified ingredient.

While the chemical defence of the nettle is only too apparent, many of our other plants use less obvious but equally powerful chemical defences. Take bracken (*Pteridium aquilinum*), for example. This ubiquitous Irish fern is just brimming with noxious chemicals.

Bracken is a well adapted pioneer species, and quickly colonises any suitable patch of bare ground.

Once it gains a foothold it spreads rapidly and can quickly dominate an area – a dominance backed up by an impressive chemical arsenal. Scientific studies in the USA have shown that bracken leaches chemicals into the soil that actively inhibit the germination of competing plant species, a process known as allelopathy. This effectively gives young bracken a head-start, and even if the competitors' seeds do eventually germinate they are no match for the already well established young bracken fronds.

Few animals eat bracken, and with good reason. Young fronds contain high concentrations of cyanogenic glycosides, and when crushed they release highly toxic hydrogen-cyanide gas. As the fronds grow the concentration of cyanogenic compounds gradually falls off and they are replaced by bitter-tasting sesqueterpines and tannins that help to dissuade larger grazers. The fronds also contain thiaminase, an enzyme that destroys vitamin B1 and causes severe vitamin deficiency and even death in some grazing mammals. Other chemicals in the plant mimic insect moulting hormones to disrupt the development of insect pests and an array of fungicidal and antibacterial chemicals guard against infection and disease. Given this formidable array of defences it's little wonder that bracken is so successful.

And bracken is by no means alone; plants routinely use chemicals to respond to all kinds of threats and to gain the upper hand in competition with other species. At first glance plants may seem static and defenceless, but they can actually detect attack by fungi, bacteria, viruses, herbivorous insects and grazing animals... and they fight back. When a threat is encountered the plant releases a distinctive blend of volatile chemicals from the damaged area. These act as a signal, triggering potent chemical counter-measures in the rest of the plant. The characteristic smell of newly mown grass is actually a chemical signal designed to prime the rest of the plant's defences against attack.

Chemical alarm signals are a widespread phenomenon in the plant kingdom, and a growing body of research shows that they also serve to alert neighbouring plants to the danger, triggering a defensive chain reaction designed to thwart the spread of pathogens and pests. Some plants can even tell the difference between being physically damaged (e.g. by trampling or cutting) and being attacked by herbivorous insects. The chemical signals released in each case are subtly different and cause markedly different responses both in the rest of the damaged plant and in neighbouring plants.

As plants have developed their array of chemical defences, so insects have evolved countermeasures that let them continue to feed on certain plants. Plants and their insect nemeses have essentially become locked in a co-evolutionary arms race: the plants generating ever more sophisticated chemical defences and the insects developing new ways to counteract them.

But even if an insect has managed to neutralise a plant's internal defence systems it doesn't necessarily render the plant helpless. Some plants call in reinforcements. In a subtle twist of the alarm-signal mechanism already described, these plants release chemical signals that attract the natural predators of their attacker. These predators use the plant's signals to track down their next meal and so help rid the plant of the unwelcome pest.

Learning more about the chemicals plants use to defend themselves has enormous potential benefits in both medicine and agriculture. Natural products, many derived from plants, account for some £9bn of annual sales in the pharmaceutical and agrochemical markets. Active substances produced by plants often have an intrinsic medical value, and examples abound of plants with medicinal properties or of medicines derived from plant extracts. Aspirin originally came from an extract of willow bark, the leaves of the foxglove (*Digitalis pupurea*) yielded a drug used to regulate heart rate, the cancer-fighting drug Taxol is produced by a variety of yew tree and extracts from the rosy periwinkle (*Vinca rosea*) help four out of every five children with leukaemia to recover. Our growing understanding of plant defences is also helping in the battle against food-crop pests, assisting in the development of more disease resistant strains and offering alternatives to our current over-dependence on environmentally damaging pesticides.

We actually know surprisingly little about the chemical makeup of our familiar native plants. Recent analysis of the bluebell (*Hyacinthoides non-scripta*), for example, revealed dozens of previously unknown alkaloids, unusual glucosides and a compound called DMDP – a chemical only found once before in a tropical bean from Costa Rica, where it is commercially cultivated and extracted as a pesticide.

So the next ground-breaking cancer drug or big agrochemical breakthrough could well be growing right under our noses. Meanwhile the plants of the Irish countryside continue to wage their chemical war.

Enemies, beware!

Atlantic Mackerel (*Scomber scombrus*)

The Atlantic mackerel is a common and widespread fish around Irish coasts. A favourite with anglers, it is often caught in great numbers during the summer when huge shoals move inshore to feed on vast numbers of herring fry and sand eel.

Mackerel is a handsome, streamlined fish that belongs to the same family as tuna. Like its larger relative the mackerel is designed for speed and agility. It is a commercially important species that is fished extensively throughout its range. It is silver underneath and the upper surface is an iridescent blue-green punctuated with attractive dark bands. The head is long, with large eyes and a large mouth that's armed with small sharp teeth. There are two dorsal fins on the back, the first originating over the middle of the pectoral fins and the second nearer the tail.

The species is a resident of the north Atlantic ocean and the Baltic, Mediterranean and Black seas. There are two main stocks in the north-east Atlantic, the North Sea stock to the east and the British Isles stock – which includes the mackerel in Irish waters – to the west.

Adult fish are usually between 35 to 46 cm (c. 14 to 18 inches) long, with some reaching lengths of up to 56 cm (c. 22 inches). They typically weigh between and 0.45 and 1.8 Kg (1 lb and 4lb). Occasionally very large mackerel are landed, like the

3.4 Kg (7.5 lb) specimen caught from the schooner *Henrietta* off the east coast of the USA in 1925.

Mackerel are pelagic, which means that they are free swimming and live their lives in the open ocean. The species is found between the surface and a maximum depth of around 1,000 metres (c. 3,281 feet). Adult mackerel spend winter in deeper water offshore, but as the water warms in spring and summer they move inshore and form huge schools containing many thousands of fish near the surface.

Because they breathe using a method known as ram ventilation mackerel have to swim constantly to ensure a continuous flow of water over their gills. Mackerel are generally most active during the day, when they feed on a small fishes like sand-eel and herring fry, as well as zooplankton (tiny crustaceans and other animals) that they filter from the water. Seeing a huge shoal of mackerel feeding at the surface on an even larger shoal of herring fry is quite a spectacle, and is not uncommon around the Irish coast during the summer months.

Spawning takes place in the open ocean, and eggs and sperm are released into the water. Each egg contains a small globule of oil that gives it buoyancy and keeps it near the surface. Once hatched the tiny mackerel feed on the larvae of minute crustaceans called copepods. As they grow they start taking adult copepods and other zooplankton. Most of the eggs, larvae and young fish will fall prey to larger predators during their time in the plankton. Those that survive grow quickly, and will reach a length of about 25cm (c. 10 inches) in their first year. Mackerel can live for up to 25 years, although in reality few will reach that age.

Like many commercial marine fish species mackerel populations are under intense fishing pressure throughout their range. During the 1960s mackerel stocks in the north-east Atlantic plummeted as a direct result of overfishing. Although mackerel populations can recover moderately quickly given the opportunity, sustained overfishing represents a very real threat to the long term prospects of this common fish species.

Jay (*Garrulus glandarius*)

The jay is one of Ireland's most striking birds with its brightly coloured pink, black, white and blue plumage. Although they are the most colourful member of the crow family, jays can be surprisingly difficult to see. They are shy, and secretive woodland birds that rarely venture far from cover.

If there are jays in the neighbourhood, however, you will invariably hear them. They are noisy birds and their distinctive harsh screeching, usually given when they're on the move, tends to betray their presence. When you hear the call look out for a colourful medium-sized bird on the wing through the trees, and particularly the flash of a distinctive white rump. Once you spot a jay there really is no mistaking it for anything else.

The adult bird is generally a pinkish-brown colour with a black tail, white throat and rump and a conspicuous blue patch on each of its black and white wings. A broad black "moustache" extends from the base of the bill down both sides of a white bib, and the white crown is streaked with black. Sexes are similar, and juvenile birds resemble the adults but tend to be fluffier in appearance and are generally redder in colour.

Jays are found in most parts of Ireland wherever there is suitable woodland habitat and are resident all year round. Although they are secretive birds they do tend to become more conspicuous in the autumn, when they often make repeated trips to collect acorns from one area and carry them to cache them elsewhere. The jay's fondness of acorns and its habit of caching food in this way mean that jays play a vital role in the establishment and maintenance of the few native oak woodlands still left in Ireland. A single bird can bury several thousand acorns each autumn – many of which will be left to germinate.

Although acorns form the bulk of a typical jay's diet, they are also known to feed on grains, invertebrates, beech nuts and sweet chestnuts. Jays also raid other birds' nests during the summer if they get the opportunity, taking eggs and young.

In spring gatherings of unpaired jays, dubbed "crow marriages", sometimes occur. These gatherings, generally consisting of thirty or so birds, offer young jays the chance to pair up. Jays start to breed in their third spring. Courtship involves a lot of posturing with wings and tail outstretched. The nest is typically a root-lined cup of twigs high in a tree in which the female will lay 5-7 pale green eggs with buff speckles on them. The male and female take turns to incubate the eggs, which will hatch at around 16 days. Both parents then work to feed the brood, which takes about 20 days to fledge. The family stay together long after the young leave the nest, with parents continuing to feed their offspring until well into the autumn. Jays only rear one brood of young per year.

Jays have been recorded attacking crows, owls, hawks and other birds that could pose a threat by mobbing them repeatedly whilst mimicking the other birds' calls to raise the alarm. They also exhibit another unusual behaviour known as "anting". A jay will sometimes seek out and actively disturb an ants nest. Once the insects are suitably riled the bird will stand in the middle of the disturbed nest allowing the ants to swarm all over its body – a sensation that your average jay seems to thoroughly enjoy!

Anticipation junkie

It was one of those calm spring days where you feel anything is possible. The Atlantic, while not quite flat, had only the tiniest of swells. Gazing out over a vast expanse of blue, a distant haze towards the horizon was the only impediment to otherwise perfect visibility. You got the sense that at any moment the peace could be shattered by... well... anything.

Sitting on a headland looking out over the sea might not sound that thrilling a pastime on the face of it. After all a view, however arresting, can only command your attention for a limited time. But it all depends on your perspective. What adds interest, for me at least, is all the stuff you can't see. Looking out, scouring the horizon from east to west and back again, I always get the feeling that something...

anything... could appear at any time.

Anticipation and potential... the drugs of choice for the wildlife junkie.

The hit: the rush of adrenaline that kicks in when you see what you're looking for is the "high", but that endorphin fuelled, pulse quickening giddiness is all too fleeting. It's the anticipation -- the certain knowledge that every movement, every scan of the binoculars, could reveal something amazing -- that's always there. It's the slow burn that fuels the obsession, and it means you never really switch off. You're always looking!

With wildlife you get no guarantees... it's an insanely unpredictable pastime. No two visits to a location are ever the same. What you're likely to encounter will depend on the season, the weather, the time of day, the temperature and a host of other variables outside your control. We use neat words like biodiversity to encapsulate the variety of species found in a particular area -- but biodiversity isn't a static concept: it's in a constant state of flux. The selection of plants, animals, birds and fungi you could see changes all the time. You never know for sure what you might find, and that not-knowing is a huge part of wildlife's appeal.

Today we were looking for cetaceans. My companion was on official business, conducting survey work for the Irish Whale and Dolphin Group. I'd tagged along on the off chance of seeing something... anything. 24 species of whales, dolphins and porpoise have been recorded in Irish waters... about seven or eight of which could reasonably turn up off a south-west headland at this time of year. This particular day though the only one to make an appearance was the smallest of them, the harbour porpoise.

I watched the small group of porpoises for a while, moving back and forth less than a kilometre from the shore, hoping they might be a precursor to more widespread cetacean activity. Then I noticed a bird, much closer in than the porpoise. I could see it was a diver, but it was far too svelte looking for the chunky great northern divers that often loiter just offshore. Red-throated diver perhaps? But no... the pattern of the plumage around the head and throat wasn't right. I checked the flanks and there was the tell-tale white patch showing above the waterline. It was a black-throated diver -- a scarce visitor to these shores, and an excellent find.

While it's always great to see something a bit rare... simply because you don't get the chance that often, wildlife watching is not all about scarcity. Common species always have the capacity to delight and surprise. Fulmars flew around us, stiff-winged masters of the turbulent air currents of the the cliff face. Like miniature albatrosses they wheeled and dove, a wonder to behold for all of their familiarity. A little further out gannets began to congregate, folding their wings to plummet spectacularly into the water, re-emerging some seconds later with a silvery prize.

A deep "cronk, cronk, cronk" made us look up as a raven cruised by a scant six feet above our heads. You don't really appreciate how big ravens are until you see one up close. Our largest crow species, ravens are impressive looking birds. The audible "swoosh" of its broad wings, the heavy set frame, jet black plumage and massive bill all contributed to a sense of poise, confidence and power. A few seconds later and the bird was gone, but the sense of wonder lingered.

I left that day elated by what I had seen, and aware that the whole experience had been heightened by what I hadn't seen... or rather by the anticipation of what I might have seen. There's always next time.

Common Newt (*Triturus vulgaris*)

The common or smooth newt is one of only three amphibian species to occur in Ireland and is probably the only truly native one. It's cousin the common frog was in all likelihood introduced sometime around 1700, and our only other amphibian, the naterjack toad, is almost certainly an interloper.

Common newts are between 7-11 cm (2.75 – 4.33 inches) long and males tend to be slightly larger than females. Females and non-breeding males are pale brown to olive green in colour and often have two darker stripes down the back. Both sexes have an orange belly (paler in the female) that's covered in black spots. During the spring breeding season the male common newt develops a continuous wavy crest that runs from the back of the head along the back and down the tail. Their markings also become more intense during the breeding season.

Because amphibians don't have watertight skin they are very susceptible to drying out. Although adult newts spend much of their lives on land, they never stray far from fresh water. They are active mainly at night, and hole up in a cool, moist locations like under old logs, stones or compost heaps during the day.

At dusk they emerge from their hiding places to forage for food. Newts feed on worms, slugs, snails, beetles and other invertebrates when on land, using their long, sticky tongue to ensnare their prey. In the water they feed on aquatic invertebrates, grabbing them with their teeth rather than using their tongue.

After spending the winter hibernating adult newts begin to emerge in late February and March, making their way back to the water in order to breed. The male newt seeks out a female and, once suitably positioned, begins wafting glandular secretions in her direction by fanning the water with his tail. Once he's attracted his mate the male deposits a small packet of sperm called a spermatophore on the substrate. The female then positions herself over the spermatophore so that it is picked up by her cloaca. A few days later she starts to lay eggs, typically from 7-12 per day, each one placed individually on the leaf of an aquatic plant which is then wrapped around the egg to conceal it from predators. She will lay from 350 to 400 eggs in total.

After 10-20 days the eggs that have survived hatch into small tadpoles with obvious feathery gills. Newt tadpoles are carnivorous and feed on a wide range of aquatic invertebrates, even eating other newt tadpoles when they get the chance. After 10 weeks or so the tadpoles metamorphose into miniature versions of the adults and before long make their way out of the water to pursue a more terrestrial existence. These young newts stay on land until they reach three years old, at which point they become sexually mature and will return to the water to breed. The average lifespan of a common newt is around 6 years – although they can live for up to 20 years.

Common newts will breed in any suitable body of fresh water. They prefer standing water with plenty of underwater and marginal vegetation. Areas like lake margins, ponds and ditches are ideal, and newts often frequent garden ponds – especially if there are no fish in residence. Outside of the breeding season newts occupy a wide range of habitats, including deciduous woodland, wet heathland, bogs, marshes, gardens, parks and farmland.

Although they are not considered threatened common newt populations are thought to be in decline throughout Europe. They are particularly susceptible to urbanisation, agricultural development and pollution of their habitat.

Long Tailed Tit (*Aegithalos caudatus*)

Few birds in Ireland are as endearing as the long tailed tit. The acrobatic antics of this small, fluffy bird with its extraordinarily long tail are a joy to behold as it flits from tree to tree. It occasionally frequents gardens, usually in small family groups, and sometimes visits peanut feeders and fat balls to supplement its diet, especially over the winter.

With its round body and incredibly long tail the long tailed tit is easy to identify. It's a gregarious little bird, usually seen in small flocks of five to twenty-or-so birds, and you're likely to hear their approach before you see them. The high 'see see see' calls, and a distinctive trilled 'tsirrup' as members of the group communicate with one another is very distinctive: once you've heard it you'll always know when a flock of long-tailed tits is in the vicinity.

The Long tailed tit is one of our smallest birds – about the size of a coal tit apart from the long tail. Adults are around 14cm (5.5 inches) long, over half of which can be attributed to the impressive tail. The bird weighs a mere 7-10 grammes (0.25-0.35 oz) and has a wingspan of 16-19 cm (6-7.5 inches).

In general appearance this is a tiny black and white bird with delicate pink and dusky tones punctuating its plumage. It has a white head with prominent black eye stripes running back down the neck. The upper parts, wings and tail are predominantly black with flashes of pink showing, while the underside is a dusky-white, also tinged with pink.

These are incredibly acrobatic little birds, and use their long tails as a counterbalance as they hang every-which-way in an incessant quest for food. In flight they look for all the world like tiny white balls on sticks as they bounce energetically from tree to tree.

Long tailed tits favour deciduous woodland, hedgerows, parks and gardens, although they are also found on heath or scrub land where there are large shrubs and bushes to provide food and cover. They feed mainly on insects, spiders and grubs, but will also take small seeds in autumn and winter.

As with other small birds, long tailed tits can suffer high mortality in cold winters. Over the winter they often roost together to help retain heat, and it's amazing how many manage to squeeze, tail and all, into a suitable tree crevice, nest box or roosting pouch.

Long tailed tits start breeding earlier in the year than other tit species. Construction of the elaborate dome-shaped nest can start as early as the end of February. The nest is an elastic structure of moss woven together with spiders webs and animal hair. The outside is usually camouflaged with lichen, while the inside lined with a layer of up to 2,000 feathers. Sited high in a tree or lower down in thorny scrub like hawthorn, gorse or bramble, this amazing structure can take the birds up to three weeks to build.

The female lays 8-12 small white eggs in the nest from March to April. Incubation takes 12-14 days and the young fledge 14-18 days later. A pair will rear one and occasionally two broods during a typical breeding season. Later in the season other long tailed tits may join a pair and help them to rear their young.

Once considered an infrequent garden visitor, garden bird surveys show that long tailed tits are becoming more common in our gardens. This increased use of gardens and a succession of relatively mild winters means that long tailed tit populations appear to be thriving – so keep an eye and an ear out for this endearing little bird in a garden

near you....

Peacock butterfly (*Inachis io*)

The large, unmistakeable eye-spots on each of the hind-wings, which resemble those on a peacock's tail, are what give this striking butterfly its name. It is one of the largest and most colourful butterflies in Ireland, and is a welcome visitor to our gardens in early spring and late summer.

The colourful, striking pattern on the wings is part of the adult butterfly's defence mechanism. When threatened the butterfly flashes its wings, exposing the eye-pattern to startle would-be predators. Persistent individuals are further dissuaded by a loud grating noise that the butterfly can produce by rasping its forewings. While the upper surface of the wings is very bold and striking, the underside is dull and cryptically marked, serving as excellent camouflage when the wings are closed and the butterfly is at rest.

Peacock butterflies emerge from hibernation during the first warm days of spring, usually sometime in early March. Males will secure a vantage point near a sunny nettle patch around mid-day and will defend it vigorously against other males. This territorial instinct is so compelling that males have been known to chase birds that stray into their patch, and will even fly up to investigate a twig or stone thrown above them. Any passing female will be chased by the territorial male and hounded for several hours until mating takes place.

The female starts to lay eggs in May, and is very particular about the plant and location. She will invariably choose the tip of a healthy stinging nettle (*Urtica dioica*) in full sunshine, and will deposit large clusters of 300-400 eggs on the underside of the young leaves.

The adults, their role in life fulfilled, will die soon afterwards. Peacock butterflies disappear for a time during June and July when one generation dies off and the next is developing in the nettle patch.

Eggs hatch 7-21 days after laying and the caterpillars create a communal tent at the top of the nettle by drawing leaves together and binding them with silk. Safe inside the caterpillars feed voraciously on the leaves that make up their refuge until they have consumed them completely. They then move on to fresh leaves, create a new retreat and begin feeding again.

Mature caterpillars are velvety black with finely speckled white dots and are covered in black spines. The caterpillars' spines are thought to deter larger predators, but offer little defence against spiders and parasitic wasps which kill a large number of them. Peacock caterpillars stay together in the nettle patch for about a month, at which point they are fully grown and disperse to pupate.

The pupa is usually suspended from vegetation up to a metre above the ground and is well camouflaged. During the 2-4 weeks spent in the pupae phase the remarkable transformation into an adult butterfly takes place.

Adult butterflies emerge from mid July onwards and begin seeking out nectar rich plants like buddleia and thistle to feed. This feeding continues until mid-September when the onset of cooler, shorter days prompts adults to take refuge in hollow trees, dark buildings and sometimes houses to wait out the rigours of winter.

Peregrine Falcon (*Falco peregrinus*)

The peregrine falcon is undoubtedly one of Ireland's most impressive birds. A large, powerful falcon it is considered by many to be the ultimate bird-of-prey, diving in a spectacular, vertical stoop to strike its quarry – other birds – in mid air. The peregrine is thought to reach speeds of up to 180 mph as it plummets earthward, though it usually levels off slightly and slows before striking its prey with outstretched talons. The razor-sharp claw of the hind-toe delivers the killing blow with the leg partially flexed on impact. Stricken prey is often allowed to drop to the ground before the raptor circles back to collect its prize.

In the summer months peregrines can be seen around the coastal cliffs, mountain crags and inland quarries on which they breed. In winter they frequent favourite hunting grounds like moorland, marshes and estuaries, where pandemonium amongst other birds often heralds the approach of these supreme aerial hunters.

The peregrine is around 45cm (17½ inches) long with a robust build. Adults are a dark, blue-grey above and white below. The breast is barred with black – with the much larger female showing more prominent barring than the male. Peregrines have a distinctive moustache of dark plumage either side of the face that stands out against the pale breast and cheeks. Juveniles have browner plumage than the adults, a less prominent moustache and have vertical streaks rather than horizontal bars below. Flight is generally a series of rapid wing-beats followed by a prolonged glide. The bird also spends long periods perched, shoulders hunched, ever watchful.

Peregrine populations were severely affected by the widespread use of organochlorine pesticides like DDT during the 1950's and 60's. At the time these pesticides were commonly added to seeds. While these seeds contained a relatively low quantity of pesticide the chemicals became concentrated in the tissues of pigeons and other birds, which ate the treated seeds in large numbers. Peregrines would then eat numerous contaminated birds, resulting in a further concentration of the pesticide in the falcons. While not always lethal to the adult birds, these high concentrations of pesticide would render them sterile or caused them to lay very brittle eggs that shattered under the weight of the female as she tried to incubate them. Peregrine numbers plummeted to dangerously low levels.

Since the 1970's a ban on these pesticides has allowed peregrine populations to slowly recover across much of their northern European range, including here in Ireland, where we now have an estimated 265 breeding pairs in the Republic and a further 100 pairs in the North. Peregrines rear a single brood of chicks each year. Between April and June the female lays three to four buff-coloured eggs with red speckles on the nest site or eyrie, typically a rocky ledge on a steep cliff-face. Incubation takes around twenty-eight days and the young birds fledge between thirty-five and forty-two days after hatching.

During the winter months peregrine numbers increase considerably as birds from further north in their range visit Ireland, following their migratory prey species south. For many people the winter months offer the best chance of spotting a peregrine as the birds patrol the skies over estuaries, mudflats and coastal waterways around the country.

Pike (*Esox lucius*)

One of coarse anglers most sought after fish, the pike often features in the classic tale of the "one that got away". The pike is one of our ultimate freshwater predators. Hidden against a backdrop of weeds this impressive fish bides its time, waiting for a likely meal to stray within range. Then it launches itself forward with awesome speed and power. Its unwitting victim becomes the pike's next meal before it even realises it's in danger.

The pike is a widely distributed fish that occurs in many northern countries, including the USA, southern Canada, the UK, Ireland, most of northern Europe, western Scandinavia, the Baltic states and Russia south to the Caspian Sea and east through southern Siberia to the Bearing Straits. It is found in still or slow-moving freshwater habitats like lakes, canals and slow-flowing sections of many rivers.

In general pike prefer well oxygenated water that offers plenty of weed cover and a neutral or alkaline pH, although they are sometimes found in more open and fast-flowing water. They also tolerate low levels of salinity and occasionally venture into brackish water.

Pike grow to be large fish can reach up to 1.5 metres (5 foot) long and weigh up 35 kg (77 lb). They have a flat, broad, almost duck-like snout and a long streamlined body on which the dorsal and anal fins are placed well back. Their colour is dependent on their environment to some extent. Specimens from very weedy water tend to be mottled green and yellow, affording them maximum camouflage amongst the underwater foliage while those from more open habitats tend to be a more uniform in colour. Fish from brackish water are generally more yellowish. All pike get darker with age, and older specimens eventually turn dark brown or grey in colour.

The pike catches its food by means of stealth, either lying concealed to ambush passing prey, or actively stalking its victim. Whichever strategy it employs the pike relies on surprise: its final attack is an explosive burst of speed that leaves the victim with little chance of escape.

Pike feed on other coarse fish, including roach, rudd, dace and perch, trout and salmon, and even smaller pike. They also take frogs, newts, crayfish, young waterfowl and small mammals.

Spawning takes place between the end of March and the beginning of May, generally in relatively shallow water. Pike often spawn in the same location each year, and the whole process can last for several weeks. The number of eggs depends on the size of the females, with large fish producing upwards of half a million eggs in a season. These eggs are sticky and adhere to underwater plants.

The young pike hatch after 10-15 days and remain attached to the plants until their yolk sacks are consumed, after which they become free swimming. At first the fry eat small invertebrates, but at about

5cm (2 inches) long they start hunting other fish fry and tadpoles.

Once they survive the early stages of their development pike grow quickly, often reaching a weight of 1 kg (2.2 lb) within 3 years. Males reach sexual maturity and are ready to breed at 2 years, females at 4 years.

Pike are relatively common fish, but like other freshwater fish they are threatened by the continued pollution of our waterways and the general deterioration of water quality throughout the state. In some European states local pike populations are threatened by overfishing. Sometimes pike are introduced to river systems or lakes for sport, and unless carefully managed this practice can have a devastating effect on the indigenous fish population.

Pygmy Shrew (*Sorex minutus*)

As its name suggests the pygmy shrew is small. In fact at just 2.5 to 6g (0.09 to 0.2 oz) in weight it is by far Ireland's smallest mammal and ranks as one of the smallest in the world. The pygmy shrew is our only shrew species, and along with the hedgehog, is one of only two insectivores (animals whose diet consists predominantly of insects and other invertebrates) found in Ireland.

Adult pygmy shrews have a body length of between 4 and 6 cm (1.6 and 2.4 inches) and a tail that's about 3-5 cm (1.2-2.0 inches). They have small eyes, a long pointed snout and long whiskers. Their body is covered with short, dense grey-brown fur that is lighter on the underside of the animal.

Because they are so small pygmy shrews have to remain active more or less constantly. Their diminutive size means that they have a high surface area in relation to their volume – and that means that despite their dense fur coat they lose heat very quickly. To compensate shrews have a very high metabolic rate, which generates the heat they need to survive, but also means they need a lot of fuel relative to their body size.

Basically for shrews resting is a dangerous business. A pygmy shrew needs to eat more than its own body weight every day to survive – and if it goes without food for more than two hours it could starve to death. Shrews have to stay active day and night, all year round.

Pygmy shrews feed on insects, spiders and other invertebrates. They seem to have a particular predilection for woodlice. When foraging they rely on their sense of smell, touch and hearing more than their eyesight, which is thought to be poor. To extract as much energy as possible from their food pygmy shrews sometimes consume their own droppings, passing the food through their stomachs a second time to absorb more nutrients.

Solitary and territorial in nature pygmy shrews don't tolerate the presence of other individuals within their territory. They hiss, make high-pitched squeaking noises, and will fight if necessary to drive away intruders. The obvious exception is when males and females come together to mate. Mating is brief, and males soon leave.

After a gestation period of 22-25 days the female gives birth to a litter of four to seven young. Births generally occur between April and September, peaking in June and July. Newborn shrews only weigh about 0.25 g (0.01 oz) but grow quickly and are fully weaned at around 22 days, when they leave to fend for themselves. Female pygmy shrews typically rear two litters each year.

Pygmy shrews don't live long, and have a maximum lifespan of about 16 months. In reality not many will make it beyond their first few months. Their small size and their need to feed constantly makes them particularly susceptible to unpredictable environmental change – like inclement weather – and sustained periods of bad weather can wipe out large numbers. They also have a host of predators that include owls, foxes, stoats and perhaps their greatest enemy, the domestic cat.

Pygmy shrews are common and widespread – occurring all over Ireland wherever there's sufficient ground cover. Despite that they are rarely seen – mainly because of their small size and secretive nature. Unfortunately the only time many of us see a pygmy shrew is when the pet cat brings one back to the house. Other threats include habitat loss, intensive

grazing and the widespread use of pesticides.

Thank you for reading *The Irish Wildlife Collection, Volume 1.*

Look out for subsequent volumes in the series soon, or if you'd like to receive an email when we publish a new volume please subscribe to the Ireland's Wildlife mailing list here:

www.irelandswildlife.com/subscribe

Please take a moment to leave a review

If you've enjoyed this book please consider

heading back over to Amazon and leaving a review to

me and other people know what you think.

About Calvin Jones

Calvin Jones is a lifelong wildlife lover, founder and managing editor of Ireland's Wildlife (www.irelandswildlife.com), and a wildlife guide for Discover Wildlife Experiences on the stunning West Cork stretch of Ireland's Wild Atlantic Way.

He started Ireland's Wildlife to share his passion, and encourage more people to engage with the natural world around them. It also has the added bonus of allowing him to head outside with a pair of binoculars and legitimately claim he is working.

Originally from the North Wales coast, Calvin now lives in an old schoolhouse in rural West Cork, Ireland with his wife, three daughters, seven chickens and an irritatingly self-assured cockerel.

Living in the country was supposed to be peaceful, but so far it's not working out that way....

Other books by Calvin Jones

Bridwatching for Beginners
An simple mini-guide to help you take your first steps in a hobby that can last a lifetime.

Choosing Binoculars for Birding and Wildlife
This simple guide cuts through the jargon and offers straightforward, practical advice to help you choose your ideal pair of binoculars.

Empire: Book One of the Bantara Chronicles
Empire is a tale of heroes and tyrants, assassins and spies that unfolds against a backdrop of civil unrest and political intrigue. It follows one woman's quest to unearth her true heritage, unlikely alliances and a chain of events that change the fate of the mighty Empire of Bantara forever.

Contents

24989362R00127

Printed in Great Britain
by Amazon